STAGEFRIGHT SOLVED
THE OFFICIAL STAGEFRIGHT SURVIVAL SCHOOL MANUAL

By
Burton Jay Rubin

With
Foreword and Postscript

By
David L. Charney, M.D.

Copyright 2013, Burton Jay Rubin
Portions Copyright 1981, 1985, 1986, 2007

TABLE OF CONTENTS

Foreword vii

Introduction ix

Chapter 1: What Causes Stagefright? 1

Chapter 2: Frequent Issues In Stagefright 15
Anticipatory Anxiety 15
Important People Are Coming and the Potted Palm Phenomenon 17
Let's Go Around The Room and Introduce Ourselves 18
What Did I Say? 20
People Could See I Was Nervous 21
The NASCAR Assumption 21
Magical Thinking 22
Distorted Thinking 23
Procrastination 25
Preparation and Presentation 26
What Do I Tell The Boss? 28
Perfectionism 29
Nonverbal Presentations 30

Chapter 3: Managing Stagefright 33

Chapter 4: Distraction Techniques for Overcoming Stagefright ... 41
Prompting 43
Staying in the Present by Contact with the Physical Environment 43
Outward Focus 45
Slowing Down 45
Taking Things Syllable by Syllable 46
Emphasis and Inflection 46
Wanting To Be There 47
Thought Stoppers 48
Floating 49
Pausing 50
Paradoxical Intention 50

Chapter 5: Going Blank and Other Special Concerns 53
Going Blank 53
Shaking Hands and Legs 54
Quivering Voice 55
Dry Mouth 56
Fainting 56

Chapter 6: Some Cognitive Adjustments ... 59
Ego Reduction ... 59
Acceptance ... 60
It's Not Always About You ... 60
Margin of Safety ... 61
Forgiving Yourself ... 62

Chapter 7: The Stagefright Medicine Chest ... 63
Placebo ... 64
Alcohol ... 65
Benadryl ... 66
Caffeine ... 67
Beta Blockers ... 67
Alprazolam ... 72
Yes, We Have No Bananas ... 73
That's Nuts ... 74
Valerian ... 75
Vitamins ... 75
Other Stuff ... 75
Meditations on Medications ... 76

Chapter 8: Drills, Skills and Exercises ... 79
Timed Readings ... 79
Skipping Lines ... 80
Eye Contact ... 84
"Caring What Other People Think About Me" Worksheet ... 86
Toastmasters ... 88
Practice and Exposure ... 89

Chapter 9: The Phantom of Van Hecke Hall ... 91

Chapter 10: Stagefright In Art and Culture ... 99
Literature ... 99
Television ... 101
Government ... 102
Cinema ... 103
Music ... 103
Please Pass the Stagefright ... 104

Chapter 11: In Session ... 109
Important People are Coming and Eye Contact ... 109
Outward Focus ... 111
Slowing Down ... 113
Medication ... 113
Going Around the Room and Introducing Ourselves and Rehearsing ... 114
Anticipatory Anxiety and the Rubber Band Technique ... 115
Going Blank ... 116

Old Habits and Forgiveness 118
Staying in the Present and Rehearsing 119
Over-Analysis and Hypnosis 122
Practicing vs. Testing 122

Chapter 12: What Doesn't Work and Why 125
The "Stickiness" Issue 126
The Power of Negative Thinking 127
Unwelcome Inner Dialogues 128
Temporal Considerations 129
Breathing 129
Don't Slouch 131
Hypnosis 131
Manipulating your Content 132
Imagining, Visualizing 134
Hurting Yourself 134
Suffering for Your Art 135
Positive Affirmations, Good Thoughts, More Visualizations 136
"Channel Your Nervous Energy" 136
The "Sarnoff Squeeze" 137
Eat Lightly, Arrive Early 138
Elaborate Preparation 138
Herbals, Botanicals and Special-Purpose Preparations 140
Getting In Touch With Early Experiences 140
Anything That Tells You to Do Something But Not How to Do It 141
Just About Everything Anybody Tells You to Do As A Stand-Alone Fix
Before Your Presentation 141
Every Other Hackneyed Cliché, Simple Step and Useless Bromide
You've Ever Heard 142

Chapter 13: The Jury Is Still Out 143
Biofeedback 143

Chapter 14: Conclusions 145

Postscript: The Stagefright Survival School Post-Graduate Course 149

Glossary 153

About the Authors 155

FOREWORD
BY DAVID L. CHARNEY, M.D.

Congratulations to Burt Rubin on this expanded version of his important book on overcoming stagefright, our term for *extreme* fear of public speaking. For more than 25 years, Burt has been the mainstay of our program, the Stagefright Survival School. Burt knows this problem intimately, having had to deal with it for himself during his own school days. After he got help for his own stagefright, he was filled with a missionary zeal to help others overcome it too. Burt anchored the early days of our program and worked energetically and passionately to strengthen and improve it over time. This book contains the culmination of his wisdom and methods for successfully overcoming the difficult problem of stagefright.

You may be wondering, "Do these guys really understand what I'm dealing with?" If you have been burdened with *extreme* fear of public speaking, let me reassure you, that yes, finally someone *really* gets it. Conquering stagefright takes someone who has personally experienced the problem, understands it deeply and is willing to tell it plain to the world. Burt Rubin is that person. People can tell right away that Burt really knows what he's talking about. Not only has he had to work through stagefright himself, Burt has developed solid explanations, techniques and therapeutic measures that actually work. He has ceaselessly refined them over the years and they are contained within this volume, making them accessible to the many who have remained painfully silent, stuck in their lives and careers because of this difficult barrier.

My role has mainly been to help those people seeking to overcome stagefright by explaining the medication support we often employ to cushion the early efforts of our students to take on their intimidating problem. I liken the medications I prescribe to training wheels. They certainly can help a person take on their first practice speeches with less anxiety, which is an encouragement that moves the process along nicely. Useful as they are, I always tell our students that the core help will come mainly from Burt and his wonderful and effective methods.

Our approach to stagefright is consistent with some of our other specialties at the Roundhouse Square Counseling Center. We try to devise helpful programs that match up to the unique requirements that specific conditions call for. In the case of stagefright, the winning combination includes: our group classes, customized cognitive-behavioral techniques and individualized counseling for each student based on Burt's deep experience along with medication support for those who want it. And now we also have Burt's book, which you're holding in your hands, to round it out.

I have been privileged to meet hundreds of our Stagefright Survival School students, since I have attended many sessions of Burt's group meetings and have had one-on-one appointments with students to initiate and adjust medication plans. I am always impressed by the courage and bravery of those who make the decision to quit hiding out and address their problems head on.

Sometimes years after graduation, I have met with some of our graduates who may have stumbled a bit and needed a refresher of attending a few of our group meetings or a renewal of their medication. They uniformly are full of praise for how our program dramatically changed their lives for the better. They tell me about the reenergized arc of their careers and about accomplishments that they never dreamed they could achieve, thanks to overcoming their *extreme* fear of public speaking. Sometimes they describe having just a little residual difficulty that needs some additional help. I came to think of these people as dealing with "The Last 10 Percent." I have contributed a final chapter to this book to convey my guidance on how to handle that.

You are fortunate to have Burt as your guide as you read his book! Armed with Burt's book, you can break through your difficult problem of extreme fear of public speaking guided by our all-knowing, wise and knowing guru!

If you want to experience the full benefit of the Stagefright Survival School, please call 877-657-8243 or 703-836-7130 or visit our website: www.StagefrightSurvival.com. The Stagefright Survival School is located in Alexandria, Virginia.

INTRODUCTION

This is the only book about stagefright that you will ever need to read. We are going to answer the two key questions that people who have stagefright have been asking since there was stagefright. These questions have never before been satisfactorily answered: "How do I know I won't get panicky during my presentation?" and "What if I get panicky during my presentation?"

The problem has been solved. While people who are severely affected by stagefright are never really "cured," this book will enable you fully to understand and successfully address ways to manage it and, at last, will provide you with your answers to those two key stagefright questions.

The information provided here represents a synthesis of the existing knowledge of the chemical mechanisms of stagefright with my own understanding of the cognitive patterns that initiate those chemical mechanisms based on more than twenty-five years of clinical experience at the Stagefright Survival School and its predecessors. I am aided in that understanding by my close, long-time collaboration with David L. Charney, M.D., a psychiatrist who, as we like to say, viewed the problem from the outside, while I experienced it firsthand, from the inside.

Over the course of those more than twenty-five years I have been privileged to have helped people from all walks of life. Physicians, even some psychiatrists, lawyers, accountants, engineers, diplomats, writers, entrepreneurs, government officials, students and people from other fields too numerous to name. Most typically I work with professionals, mid-level managers on their way up and entrepreneurs just meeting with success and encountering the need to give presentations on a recurring basis. These are people who find that they can no longer hide their lights under the proverbial "bushel basket."

The comprehensive model presented here will enable you to better understand the origins and roots of stagefright, which lie in certain patterns of thinking; where the "switches" are for turning on the chemical reactions that result in stagefright; and how to keep your mental finger off those switches.

I have provided the basis for challenging certain kinds of distorted thinking that tends to perpetuate stagefright, along with a discussion of stagefright in art and culture, to provide a perspective. I have also laid out specific distraction techniques to enable you to clear your mind of the self-conscious thoughts about potential embarrassment that set off the chemical stampede.

I also discuss medications that are useful to counter the effects of the body's naturally released catecholamines, which are responsible for the physical and emotional discomfort experienced during stagefright. Finally, I attempt to debunk some of the fallacious, ridiculous and even harmful advice that circulates so plentifully around this subject.

I hope to have provided a useful, supportive reference and text for people who are seeking professional help. For people without access to professional resources or who have lesser degrees of anxiety, I hope to provide a kind of "industrial strength" self-help.

A special word about stagefright as it affects two professional groups is in order. The one group we see in great numbers, the other very rarely. They are lawyers and musicians. Lawyers easily constitute the single largest occupational group in our program. It may well be that this is because we are located in the Washington, D.C. suburbs where your chances of encountering a lawyer walking down the street are somewhat greater than your chances of encountering someone wearing a wristwatch. However, we think it is not our location; we think that the method of training lawyers is very likely to exacerbate the preexisting obsessive-compulsive tendencies we believe to be common among them and potentially cause anxiousness that can develop into stagefright.

The other group is musicians. While I have worked with several musicians over the years, their number is small. Nevertheless, the literature reflects that professional musicians are one of the largest occupational groups that suffer from stagefright. Some reports indicate that as many as 50 percent of professional musicians take medication to address their problem. Sadly, a very high percentage is also said to self-medicate with alcohol.

While the distraction techniques I have laid out are specifically directed to the public speaking experience, and some are simply unavailable in other performance contexts, these discussions and principles should be helpful to performers as well as others. The key in all cases is to distract yourself from thoughts of potential embarrassment and from self-conscious awareness, focusing exclusively on presentation content.

The key to tightrope walking is said to be, "Don't look down." The key to managing stagefright is to not think about yourself while presenting. With some people, these kinds of thoughts can be persistent and compelling so it may become necessary to distract yourself by employing a technique to redirect your attention into the content you're presenting. We hope you will find the tools you need here to make your fear of public speaking a thing of the past.

It is our intention that this book become an integral part of our Stagefright Survival School curriculum for those able to join us and that it will serve as a "substitute teacher" for those unable to do so.

Burke, Virginia
July, 2013

CHAPTER 1
WHAT CAUSES STAGEFRIGHT?

Anyone who has experienced stagefright knows that it is an overwhelming dread of speaking or presenting a nonverbal demonstration of some sort in front of an audience, which can consist of as few as just one other person. The dread is accompanied by powerful physical reactions, which typically include a racing heart, rapid breathing (hyperventilating), tremulousness, shaking or wobbly arms or legs and a quivering voice to name a few. What is less well known is that in a very important sense, stagefright has relatively little to do with performing before an audience. It is, in essence, a chemical problem caused by the production of a family of chemicals called catecholamines.

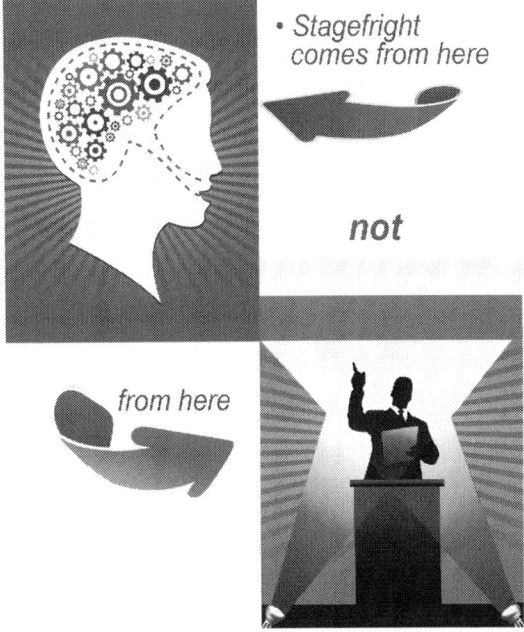

Catecholamines are extremely powerful stimulants. They are released into the bloodstream as hormones and also travel through the nervous system as chemical messengers called neurotransmitters. The most widely known member of the family, familiar to anyone who has ever watched a television hospital drama, is adrenaline, also known as epinephrine.

At some point in a typical hospital TV show, a character whose heart has stopped is brought in on a gurney and someone yells, "Quick, get me an ampoule of epi!" and after much heroic effort, the patient in cardiac arrest is duly revived. That's how powerful stimulant members of the catecholamine family are — they can revive people who have no heartbeat. Clearly no amount

CHAPTER 1: WHAT CAUSES STAGEFRIGHT?

of "epi" is going to help Aunt Martha who passed away some years ago, but you can imagine the effect of such powerful stimulants on someone trying to appear calm while giving a talk.

The purpose of these chemicals is to initiate your "fight or flight" response, which is a physiological reaction that happens when you encounter a dangerous situation. In its appropriate place, this is a good thing and can, and probably has, saved your life. If you are tired while driving home at night and get a little too close to the car in front of you and see its brake lights come on, you will get a jolt of catecholamines to wake you up, which will get you to maintain a safe distance and stay alert until you can get safely home.

Catecholamines exercise their stimulant properties in a number of different ways. Your breathing may become rapid and shallow. Your heart will begin to beat more rapidly and forcefully, which would be a good thing if you faced physical danger. The heart pumps blood, which carries oxygen and nutrients throughout the body. Oxygen and nutrients are needed in order for your muscles to produce movement. Faced with real danger and the need to fight or run away, it is beneficial for your muscles to receive extra oxygen and nutrients.

Here again, catecholamines provide your muscles with enhanced oxygenation enabling a faster more forceful response. At the same time, the stimulant effect causes your muscles to start to contract against each other, essentially taking the slack out of the system, to provide for a quicker fight or flight response. Muscles are like cables — they can only pull, they can't push. For this reason each muscle has an opposing or opposite muscle to reverse its action. For instance, you have a biceps muscle to pull your forearm up. And, so you don't end up stuck that way, you also have a triceps to straighten it back out again. Because the stimulant effect of the catecholamines is felt by all the skeletal muscles of the body, the biceps starts contracting against the triceps and vice versa. This is experienced as the tremulousness or shaking of stagefright and gives rise to such common descriptions of fear as "I was shaking like a leaf."

You may have wondered what sort of lousy engineering goes into a human being that makes you shake just when you are being challenged and need to function at your best. In reality, you are experiencing your opposing muscles squeezing against each other, tightening things up, in response to catecholamine stimulation as part of your fight or flight response.

Because you also have some muscular tissue in your throat, that tightens up as well, resulting in the cracking voice or involuntary swallowing that some people with stagefright experience.

Some other people experience what is commonly referred to as butterflies in the stomach. This is a real phenomenon and is one of the effects of the release

CHAPTER 1: WHAT CAUSES STAGEFRIGHT?

of catecholamines. You didn't swallow a moth, of course; you are feeling the constricting of the blood vessels of the internal organs as more blood is directed to the skeletal muscles where it is needed to carry oxygen and nutrients as part of the fight or flight response. Commenting on this phenomenon, Helen Hayes, the First Lady of the American Theater famously observed: "Of course, I get butterflies before I go on stage. But now I have them flying in formation."

The physical reactions of stagefright are really nothing more than exactly what we would expect from the release of the powerful catecholamine stimulant chemicals if you were threatened in some fashion that had called forth your fight or flight responses. Indeed, it has been hypothesized that if a sufficient dose of the same substances that stagefright-sufferers produce naturally could be administered to the most experienced, poised and calm of speakers, that person would experience many of the symptoms familiar to those with stagefright.

Of course, these are the very same reactions we don't want an audience to observe and attribute to us. In this sense, stagefright has been referred to as "a self-poisoning with one's own catecholamines." [1] At the same time, it is important not to make too much of this thought. It is not necessary, for example, to call 911. These are your own natural chemicals, which are rapidly destroyed and will not, for the most part, hurt you. They are responsible, however, for the distress, avoidance and disadvantage in work and social situations experienced by people with stagefright.

We've established that the physical reactions of stagefright are caused by the same chemicals that would be produced, and are designed to help us, when we are in real physical danger. But what does giving a talk have to do with being in actual physical danger?

We judge whether we are in danger against an integrated sense of self. That is, we don't think of ourselves as a collection of body parts walking around; we think of ourselves as a complete whole. We don't think, "That tractor-trailer is coming over into my lane and will crush my left arm." We think, "I am about to be hurt."

On account of this method of judging whether we are in danger, the same fight or flight responses that are activated when we are in physical danger are also activated when we are in what we might call "social danger." That is, if you think that you will embarrass or humiliate yourself and somehow diminish yourself in the eyes of others, then you are telling yourself that you are about to be hurt in a way that your body and its fight or flight mechanisms cannot distinguish from actual, physical danger.

---

[1] This description appears in the brilliant landmark work done by the Brantigan Brothers, et al., "Effect of Beta Blockade and Beta Stimulation on Stage Fright," *The American Journal of Medicine*, January 1982.

CHAPTER 1: WHAT CAUSES STAGEFRIGHT?

This emotional equation of embarrassment and loss of self-esteem with injury and even death is so basic and unconscious that the body reacts with its protective devices of fear and avoidance, just as it would to avoid an injury.

Indeed, anyone who has experienced a panic episode while giving a presentation knows just how painful that experience can be. Equating embarrassment and loss of self-esteem with injury and death is so basic that the body essentially cannot distinguish between the two.

Some years ago I worked with someone who was convinced that he had experienced a noticeable panic attack while giving a presentation at work. So deep was his sense of humiliation that he quit his job the very next day, sold or shipped his belongings and moved from the West to the East coast without any particular employment prospects. With this degree of shame and humiliation felt afterward, there is no surprise at his profound degree of dread that the experience would be repeated.

The most dramatic confirmations of this have come from military or law enforcement members who also suffered from stagefright. These were very

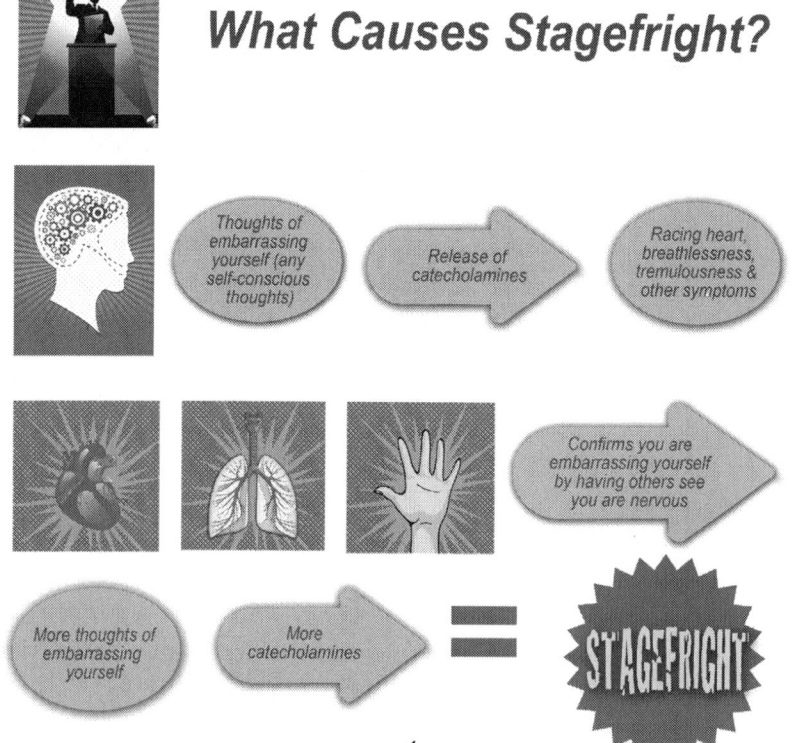

CHAPTER 1: WHAT CAUSES STAGEFRIGHT?

brave people used to confronting serious physical danger but disabled by fear at the prospect of giving a presentation.

A while back I worked with a civilian employee of one of the big departments of the federal government. He told me about his experience as a young sailor on December 7, 1941, the day that President Roosevelt called the "day that shall live in infamy" — the day Pearl Harbor was attacked. "I was there," he said. "The enemy planes were coming right overhead. They were coming toward me! They were dropping bombs; they were dropping bombs on me!" Still, he told me, "I would rather go back there than do this briefing I have coming up at work."

Similarly, I once worked with a Supervisory Special Agent of the FBI who described a shootout he had been in just a few days before. "We were on one side of this brick wall," he said, "and they [the other guys] were on the other. They were shooting at us, and we were shooting at them. I'd rather do that all over again than give this talk I have to give to my staff next week."

I have worked with FBI Special Agents, U.S. Marshals and members of the armed forces, and many of them say the same thing. Their undeniable bravery and ability to handle serious physical danger was not able to protect them from their stagefright or keep them from experiencing, when giving presentations, the same physical reactions that a civilian would experience if faced with the real dangers that the armed forces or Special Agents might face on any work day.

Thoughts of appearing nervous in front of an audience are the most common ones that stagefright-sufferers have, but any self-critical ruminations or associations are sufficient to initiate the stagefright process. The kinds of thoughts that cause the release of catecholamines activating the body's fight or flight responses are generally of this nature: "Wouldn't it be awful if I made a fool of myself?" "Wouldn't it be awful if everyone could see how nervous I am?" "Wouldn't it be awful if I became panicky and had to leave?" In short, the thoughts that stimulate the fight or flight response are fears that you will be judged harshly in some way and thereby be embarrassed or humiliated. These thoughts do not have to be prolonged, elaborate or even complete. Even a moment's association with this way of thinking is sufficient to cause the release of catecholamines.

Another fear-thought that can occur is the fear of going blank: that you will start your presentation and not remember a word of what it is you were supposed to say. Then there is the opposite response to going blank. Some people are afraid that they will blurt out something outrageous and totally inappropriate. Therefore, we can go so far as to say that **any self-conscious thought while talking to others is sufficient to cause your body to react as if you were at risk of being harmed.**

CHAPTER 1: WHAT CAUSES STAGEFRIGHT?

These fear-thoughts may occur several weeks or even months before a presentation ("anticipatory anxiety") or at the beginning, in the middle or end of the presentation itself. Anytime you tune out your presentation and tune into yourself, you are likely to experience the physical symptoms of stagefright.

Is this really possible? Can what you are thinking cause your body to release chemicals? The answer is an unequivocal "yes." In fact, there are any number of physiological mechanisms that work just this way.

If you think intensely about food, you will produce saliva, even though there may actually be no food anywhere around. If you think sad thoughts, you may produce tears, a mixture of chemicals that protects and lubricates the eyes, even though no one actually poked you in the eye. If you think you will embarrass yourself in front of one or more other people, you may produce the same chemicals that would be released if you were in physical danger.

Typically the cycle goes like this: You have the thought that you might embarrass or humiliate yourself. As soon as you have that thought, you have told yourself you are in danger and your body reacts in the only way it can — by releasing its fight or flight chemicals. Those chemicals then produce all the physical symptoms of fear. This in turn provides instant confirmation of the thought that you are about to embarrass yourself, thereby completing the circle. At the same time, the whole pattern is reinforced, causing it to spiral upward.

Because this is a circular pattern (for example, you have the thought that you might embarrass yourself by appearing nervous then the next second you actually get more nervous), it is very hard to break. That is why people with stagefright are very rarely able to help themselves out of it. **The thought of being nervous in front of an audience is a self-fulfilling prophecy.**

How do we know that we are right about all this and have developed an accurate model of what causes stagefright and upon which an effective response can be based? The answer is that our understanding of the cognitive pattern that causes stagefright has been confirmed to us hundreds of times over decades of practical, hands-on experience. Over that time, we have described to hundreds of new clients who we have just met the thought-process by which they initiate their stagefright. In each case, they have recognized and identified with it so we know we are right on target. On the other hand, had we suggested that stagefright was caused, say, by eating asparagus, we would have undoubtedly been informed on numerous occasions that the person did not consume that particular vegetable so we could not possibly know what we were talking about.

In most cases, stagefright proves to be a one-time learning experience. Once you have the experience of concluding that an audience has seen that you were panicky, you're pretty much hooked. Each time thereafter, when you have a presentation to give, you are very likely to ask yourself "How do I know it won't happen again?" Because you have no convincing, reassuring answer to that question, the cycle tends to repeat itself.

While stagefright can occur at any point in life, it most commonly derives from early school experiences. We believe it establishes itself quite readily in vulnerable people who tend to be bright, obsessive-compulsive perfectionists.

When a student lacking these characteristics is required to make a presentation in front of the class, say reciting the *Gettysburg Address*, she experiences the nearly universal nervousness that accompanies such a situation. But, lacking the predisposing traits, she is more or less able to accept that she may appear a little nervous or perhaps make a mistake. The perfectionist student, on the other hand, finds it unacceptable to appear nervous in front of the class, thereby feeling at great risk from the start. Then, should the thought occur, "I hope nobody can tell I'm nervous," she is likely to react far more profoundly, initiating the cascade of thoughts and chemicals that can result in an actual panic episode.

Perfectionists are also far more likely to have other self-critical thoughts and associations that can contribute to stagefright. A non-perfectionist is far more likely to accept the occasional stumbles and missed words that are an inevitable part of giving a presentation. The perfectionist dreads them.

In point of fact, it is practically impossible to read from a page of text without missing or mispronouncing a word. The reason for this lies in physics and engineering. The process by which we look at the ink blots on a page that we call "type" and turn them into recognized letters and words is essentially electro-*chemical*. It takes place at something approaching the speed of light. On the other hand, the process by which we vocalize those words when we speak is electro-*mechanical*; it involves the moving parts of the tongue, mouth, lips, jaw and larynx. Electro-mechanical processes are always inherently slower than electro-chemical processes. If you had a very fast computer doing the word recognition but it was hooked up to a slower printer, in this case speaking those words, then inevitably, data would get lost or damaged through that interface. That's what happens when you read out loud.

The prospect of mispronouncing a word, leaving something out or making some other mistake in the course of giving a presentation, such as displaying any sort of nervousness, is unacceptable to the perfectionist. Thus the perfectionist is, in addition, intolerant of his own level of anxiety, including the nearly universal background level of nervousness common to almost anyone giving an important presentation. The perfectionist thereby regards himself as at greater risk in giving the presentation and is therefore more likely than the non-perfectionist to initiate the chemical reactions that cause stagefright, to experience them more intensely and to sustain them for a longer period. In this way, perfectionism can

CHAPTER 1: WHAT CAUSES STAGEFRIGHT?

be thought of as the backbone on which the stagefright cycle is built or, perhaps, the glue that holds it together.

Over the years we have had students from many different walks of life at our Stagefright Survival School. We recognize, of course, that our student population does not represent a scientific sampling of the entire population that might experience stagefright. Our Washington, D.C., metropolitan-area location undoubtedly contributes to the high number of mid-career government employees we work with (although we do offer intensive weekend sessions for out-of-towners). At the same time, we see almost as many people whose motivation to be more comfortable in presentation situations is social — wedding toasts and church activities are commonly cited — as often as work-related occasions.

People who think that they might experience nervousness in a presentation situation but do not expect to be called on to actually give a presentation rarely seek help. In a real sense, they simply do not have a problem.

Our single biggest occupational group consists of lawyers. This may be due in part to the ant-like precision that is often required of them and the perfectionist mindset so many attorneys are believed to possess. I remember on one occasion receiving a letter on the stationery of the Virginia State Bar about an up-coming election. Down the side of the letterhead were listed the members of the Bar's governing council. Of approximately a dozen or so members of that statewide body, I recognized about a third as having been to our school.

Stagefright is classified by psychiatrists as a phobia, an irrational fear, and in particular as a "social phobia." It is said to make up the greater portion of all social phobias. My favorite story involving the role of perfectionism in social phobias involves the patient who approached her psychiatrist, obviously deeply troubled. When the doctor inquired as to the source of the patient's immediate distress, the patient replied, "Well, Doctor, remember when you told me that in order to get better I was going to have to learn to accept mistakes and, in fact, that I was going to have to make a mistake?" The psychiatrist replied, "Yes." "Well," said the troubled patient, "I was hoping you would help me decide just what was the very best possible kind of mistake to make."

In order for the pattern of self-conscious thoughts about embarrassing yourself to cause your body to release catecholamines, the thoughts must be convincing. Unless you genuinely convince yourself that you are at real risk of embarrassment, the reaction will not take place.

Essentially then, the difference between someone with stagefright and someone without it is that the non-affected person may be a little nervous when starting a

CHAPTER 1: WHAT CAUSES STAGEFRIGHT?

presentation but soon becomes absorbed in doing it. At that point she has no fear thoughts and so is not reacting with danger-appropriate physical reactions.

On the other hand, when vulnerable people give a presentation and they have the thought or association that they are in danger of being embarrassed or have self-critical thoughts of being judged harshly, their bodies will react with danger-appropriate physical reactions and they will experience stagefright. In this sense, stagefright-sufferers may be thought of as being more intolerant of their own anxiety than others.

Not infrequently, much to other participants' surprise, we will have someone join a class who teaches high school. How can a person who makes a living, day in day out talking in front of a group of high school kids have stagefright? (Personally, I'd be reluctant to speak to a group of high school kids without a whip and a chair.) The answer is that in that situation, in their own classrooms, doing what they do every day, teachers do not regard themselves as at risk. Teachers feel in control in their own environment; they don't feel as though they are in danger and will not initiate the fight or flight responses.

Typically, the reason such teachers come to our school is because they are facing Open School Night or some other parent-teacher event at which they fear appearing nervous in front of a parent. The same people who can spend all day talking to a bunch of potentially unruly teenagers with no discomfort can suffer from stagefright when talking to docile middle-aged parents. In this situation, the teacher has thought something along the lines of: "Wouldn't it be awful if I appeared nervous when talking to the parents? They would think what kind of teacher gets so nervous? They might complain to the principal, jeopardizing my career." Because the teacher has now convinced himself that he is in real danger, his body will respond to those thoughts with the release of catecholamines, initiating the reactions of stagefright.

Perhaps even more amazing is that from time to time we actually get people in our school who are active in local theater. Their hobby is acting and they willingly put themselves into situations of giving performances in front of other people. You can imagine the reaction of their classmates when they learn that one of their fellow stagefright-sufferers has a hobby of giving performances, without any compulsion from work or otherwise, for the pure personal pleasure it gives them. How can they need help with stagefright?

The answer is that when in character, they simply do not feel at risk of embarrassing themselves and so do not experience stagefright in that particular situation. These same actors come to our school for much the same reason as everyone else. Without the benefit of costume and makeup, when they have to give a presentation at work, they are subject to the panic of stagefright.

CHAPTER 1: WHAT CAUSES STAGEFRIGHT?

How likely we are to believe that we are at great risk and how likely our bodies are to react as if we were in actual danger when giving a presentation is therefore directly related to how much we care. The more that people have taken the life message that they must succeed and that flaws, including nervousness, are unacceptable, the more anxiety they are likely to experience in a public speaking situation. It is ironic that the more we care and the more we want to do a really good job, the more nervous and less effective we become as presenters.

Stagefright also shares a good deal in common with claustrophobia, the fear of confined spaces. In fact, stagefright can be thought of as the social equivalent of claustrophobia. Claustrophobic people are subject to fear culminating in panic when they are physically confined. The person with stagefright is reacting much the same way when he is socially confined. Although it may be physically possible to do so, there is a strong inhibition against simply leaving when you are the one called upon to give a presentation. This inhibition can create a trapped feeling not unlike what the claustrophobic person experiences when physically confined in a tight space.

The thought patterns of the two phobias share much in common as well. When a claustrophobic person is physically confined, he will have thoughts of being unable to get out, even though at that moment there is no need to do so. This thought of being trapped, perhaps with a "what if" about needing to get out thrown in, is one of those fear-thoughts that causes the body to release catecholamines initiating the fight or flight responses. Now the claustrophobic person is feeling and thinking about being trapped and, in addition, is experiencing the racing heart, rapid breathing and other fear symptoms he would experience if he were trapped and really needed to get out in a hurry. As in stagefright, these physical symptoms confirm to the claustrophobic that he is really in danger.

Similarly, in stagefright, you may feel trapped, unable to leave because of the social constraint of your obligation to give your presentation. This thought of being trapped, perhaps coupled with a thought of not knowing how you will be able to stay to complete your task, is a catecholamine-inducing fear-thought, resulting in a racing heart and the other fear symptoms. All that uncomfortable physiology confirms that you might actually have to leave, sending you on that familiar stagefright spiral.

Sometimes, stagefright-sufferers may have the fear-thought that they will say something bizarre or totally inappropriate when addressing an audience. This in turn may cause them to try and listen to themselves as they speak, in a kind of "self-censorship." Inevitably this kind of turning inward and tuning out the present increases anxiety and can lead to noticeable panic. Stagefright shares this fear of engaging in a bizarre act with several other phobias.

CHAPTER 1: WHAT CAUSES STAGEFRIGHT?

People with acrophobia, a fear of heights, may fear that they will be unable to control an impulse to throw themselves off a high place. A person with a fear of heights is not drawn to hurtling herself earthward, but totally repulsed by the idea. It is not a case of a lack of control, but of over control. The fight or flight reaction is activated in response to thinking about an impulse that does not exist. As we have discussed, fight or flight swings into action in response to thinking about being harmed even when there is no real danger present. In fact, phobic people never engage in the feared behavior. An acrophobic person will never jump off a high place or open the door of an aircraft in flight or do anything of that nature.

Although heights are not my own preferred environment, on a number of occasions in working with acrophobic people I have taken their hands and offered to jump or fall with them if that is what they thought they might do. Happily, I have never had any takers.

To be clear, let me say that there are people with various disorders who may harm themselves in that way and I certainly would not want to extend that offer to them. However, a person with a fear of heights will never throw himself from a high place on account of that fear. Similarly, a person with stagefright who fears blurting out something outrageous is highly unlikely ever to do that as a result of that condition.

In short, people with phobias never engage in feared, bizarre behavior. However, this assurance of not saying something outrageous must be differentiated from the fear of becoming panicky. Through the mechanisms I have discussed, people with stagefright certainly can become visibly panicky before an audience.

Despite the common tendency of people with stagefright to think of it as "something coming over them" as if it originated from outside rather than inside their own bodies or as having some sort of an "anxiety attack," something they carry around all the time and that flares up periodically, nothing could be further from the truth. These sensations are, in actuality, the predictable physiological responses to the anxious person's own thoughts. **Reduced to its minimum, stagefright occurs when catecholamines are released in response to fear-thoughts, which can really be any self-conscious thought you have, while talking to someone else.**

Now for some good news — and some bad news. First the bad news. How nervous you feel is due to the chemicals you are producing right then in response to your thinking; each presentation is a different experience. If you aren't prepared to apply the distraction techniques discussed later, you can have a bad experience at any time.

And now the good news. Because each time is a different experience, if you apply your distraction techniques to manage your thinking so you don't produce

CHAPTER 1: WHAT CAUSES STAGEFRIGHT?

as much of the catecholamines, you can have a good experience even after many bad experiences.

This also means that stagefright tends to be something of an ongoing problem because a triggering fear-thought can pop up at any time and, if you are not prepared to quickly displace it by using a distraction technique, you can initiate the chemical sequence that results in the fight or flight response.

Of course, the more successful experiences you have, the harder it becomes to convince yourself you are in danger during a subsequent presentation and the less "sticky" the thoughts of potential embarrassment become. Even though it takes many good experiences to outweigh even a single bad experience, no one can take from you the knowledge you have acquired about stagefright and how to manage it. Also, the more you practice using your techniques, the more adept you will become at using them should the stray thought of embarrassing yourself pop up while you are presenting.

Any kind of discomfort, such as having a cold or being hungry or some outside concern, has the potential to draw your thoughts inward while you are giving a presentation, making it more likely that you will "spike" a fear-thought and think about embarrassing yourself, causing the release of catecholamines. It is important therefore always to be prepared to use your techniques and to have your "prompting" on hand, which is the written word or phrase that reminds you to use your techniques immediately upon sensing that first up-tick in your anxiety levels. We'll discuss more about prompting later.

Without making too much of the comparison, it is also helpful for people with stagefright to think of their problem somewhat in the same way that people with an alcohol problem think about theirs. In both cases, the problem tends to be an ongoing one. Just as people with a drinking problem should not drink alcohol, people with stagefright must be careful not to start thinking about themselves when they are giving a presentation. Just as people with a drinking problem probably need to continue to go to their meetings, people with stagefright also need to go to meetings and find as many opportunities to practice presenting as possible.

Because of the continuing nature of stagefright, I prefer to think in terms of overcoming or managing it rather than of "curing" it. The important thing is to be able to function without disadvantaging yourself, having to turn down a job opportunity or promotion, being able to compete on the basis of your knowledge and skills and not losing sleep or enduring needless suffering.

Sometimes people with stagefright have an additional dread. They fear that not only will they embarrass themselves but that they will spread their stagefright to

CHAPTER 1: WHAT CAUSES STAGEFRIGHT?

others. In addition to harming themselves socially, they will also thereby harm other people, thus turning themselves into true pariahs. You can imagine how profound the unwillingness to face an audience is for someone who is convinced that not only that he will be humiliated, but who also harbors the secret shame that he can spread his discomfort like a plague.

Although people with stagefright commonly think of themselves as having a "disease" and a recurrent one that flares up when they are called upon to address an audience, there is no infectious agent involved. They are simply turning on their own fight or flight responses when they do not want to do so. As we have previously discussed, people who are most susceptible to severe stagefright are obsessive-compulsive perfectionist sorts of people who are unable to experience the normal level of anxiety that usually accompanies appearing before an audience. Because they are unwilling to appear even a little nervous, they are fearful that it will show and, of course, that fear initiates their fight or flight responses. Therefore we know that obsessive-compulsive perfectionism is a risk factor for stagefright. That risk factor is transmissible, too: you get it from your parents or others who raised you in a belief system that over-emphasized safety, disdained mistakes and failures, avoided risks and were critical of any outcome that was not the best.

It may be possible that a stagefright-prone person might not have the fear-thought that she will embarrass herself in front of an audience the first several times she speaks in public. However, she may have the thought pop into her mind one day down the road after having delivered many successful speeches and, from that day on, she will suffer from stagefright. This may explain why, although we typically see people who have had stagefright from their early school days, it sometimes doesn't develop until later in life, such as in college or graduate school or after people have started a career.

It is also possible that for such people, exposure to someone who has stagefright or who panics during a presentation may in fact be a precipitating event. It is fair to ask the question, "Can you catch stagefright from someone else?" The answer is: sort of, maybe, it depends.

It could be said that someone could catch stagefright from another person only if she were predisposed in the first place. It is probably wise therefore for people with stagefright not to make too much of it in front of their children or other people who may be susceptible to the suggestion of appearing panicky in front of an audience.

When, however, you are assigned to do a presentation, all bets are off. You have been made to give the presentation and therefore you are not responsible for the consequences. Regrettable though it may be to some stagefright-sufferers,

CHAPTER 1: WHAT CAUSES STAGEFRIGHT?

you cannot be put into quarantine so that you never face an audience. On the contrary, you need to learn what causes stagefright, what you need to do to overcome it and then face and manage the fear.

CHAPTER 2
FREQUENT ISSUES IN STAGEFRIGHT

Certain issues arise repeatedly in dealing with and treating stagefright. This is not very surprising considering the thoughts that trigger it and the common personality traits that most people who have it share. In addition, both workplace and social environments tend to create similar presentation situations that recur frequently.

ANTICIPATORY ANXIETY

Anticipatory anxiety is the worry felt from immediately before to as long as weeks or even months before a presentation. It is often accompanied by a racing heart and some of the same physical reactions that are experienced in a presentation situation. As we've discussed, your body cannot differentiate an actual physical injury from the social or emotional injury of embarrassing or humiliating yourself. If you picture an upcoming presentation event and have a fear-thought like "Wouldn't it be awful if I made a fool of myself?" your body will respond by releasing catecholamines and activating your fight or flight responses, even if the actual presentation may be weeks away.

Again, remember: Think about food and you will produce saliva to begin to digest your meal, even though there is no food around. Think about embarrassing yourself during a presentation and you will produce catecholamines just as if you were in actual physical danger at that moment.

Several things can contribute to and reinforce the habit of long-term anticipatory anxiety, such as picturing, daydreaming about or obsessing about a planned presentation weeks before the actual event. Control is an important aspect to people with stagefright. This need for control may take the form of wanting to be able to arrange things in certain ways and wanting to be certain of the outcome of events. The only place people can completely achieve this sort of control, of course, is in their own minds. Thus, a person with stagefright might find herself — weeks in advance — picturing what the room will be like, how it will be arranged and even who will sit where.

Because this kind of daydreaming is accompanied by real feelings of excitement from catecholamine release, the habit tends to become reinforced, even though the experience is a negative one. It's like poking new dental work with your tongue or continuing to touch an injury even though it may hurt when you do so.

Another possible reinforcement for the long-term anticipatory anxiety habit may come from a kind of subtle "magic thinking" that some people may engage in.

CHAPTER 2: FREQUENT ISSUES IN STAGEFRIGHT

At some level there may be a sense that, "If only I think about it enough and worry about it enough in advance, maybe those panicky feelings won't sneak up on me when I do my presentation." In other words, "If I suffer enough now by way of anticipating my presentation, maybe it won't go so badly."

This kind of thinking can be easily supported by one of the ways we learn. People tend to assume causal relationships between things that happen in sequence until that assumption is shown to be baseless. This tendency lies at the root of a joke about a man crumpling up paper and tossing it around a room. A visitor asks him what he is doing. The man replies "I'm crumpling up paper and throwing it around the room to keep away the elephants." "I don't see any elephants," the visitor responds. "Good system, isn't it?" the man answers.

This joke is amusing precisely because we recognize at the same time both the absurdity of the situation and the surface plausibility of the paper crumpler's logic. In this same way, many people who experience anticipatory anxiety may believe that they have a good system that is best not changed or tampered with. They have experienced long-term anxiety before giving a talk on previous occasions. One way or another, they survived the experience. When again faced with the prospect of having to speak publicly, they may return to this familiar, although painful, pattern of anticipatory fear-thinking. On some level, they have come to believe that if they don't go through this anticipatory anxiety preparation, they may not survive their next speech.

In actuality, nothing could be further from the truth. The only thing that determines the fear you will experience in giving a presentation is the catecholamines that you produce. The thinking that gives rise to anticipatory anxiety is incapable of conferring any protective benefit. All you are doing is rehearsing and reinforcing the fear-thinking that is the cause of stagefright, giving yourself an unnecessary, uncomfortable and negative experience.

Anticipatory anxiety, in reality, has no payoff. You can suffer terribly with anticipatory anxiety and have a comfortable presentation. You can suffer terribly with anticipatory anxiety and have an awful time giving the presentation. You can be free of anticipatory anxiety and have a comfortable presentation. You can be free of anticipatory anxiety and have a terrible time giving the presentation. **The anticipation and the presentation are not connected in any fashion.** Therefore, you might as well spare yourself the discomfort of the anticipation.

Interestingly enough, some people with stagefright experience only anticipatory anxiety. Once they actually begin their presentation they become so absorbed in what they are doing that they do not have fear-thoughts and thus do not trigger their fight or flight responses.

Ultimately, the solution for anticipatory anxiety takes care of itself. Like an accordion, anticipation collapses on itself and can't be sustained as you gain confidence in using your distraction techniques and as you have more frequent comfortable experiences when giving presentations. Nevertheless, because it is a particularly unnecessary kind of suffering that can include all the uncomfortable physiological responses as if you were actually in a public speaking situation, plus the inability to sleep at night, sometimes it is necessary to address it directly.

In addition, anticipatory anxiety can result in procrastination because working on a presentation represents a commitment to doing it. On occasion, this procrastination can have a serious impact in the workplace if people who are otherwise highly conscientious and responsible put off preparing for an upcoming presentation.

Now that you know the futility of anticipatory anxiety, you may wish to try one of the distraction techniques for dealing with anticipation to stop the process. See Chapter 4 for some helpful "thought stopper" techniques.

IMPORTANT PEOPLE ARE COMING AND THE POTTED PALM PHENOMENON

Another issue that arises frequently with stagefright is what to do when "really important people" are going to be present. Perhaps your boss will be there, or someone who can make a crucial evaluation. Does it really make any difference if these really important people are going to be in the audience? People whose evaluation could actually have an impact on your future? We would probably have to say yes, there is more at stake in giving this presentation than otherwise might be the case. Unfortunately that information is also entirely useless.

Thinking about the importance of a particular presentation is unlikely to add to your poise and comfort on that occasion. On the contrary, you are telling yourself you are at greater risk because of the importance of the event. When you do that, you intensify the message of danger sent to the body and you increase the stagefright process. That's why we can say that although it may be true that a particular presentation is of greater importance than usual, that information is useless. The information is unlikely to be used in any constructive fashion and is very likely to make you more nervous. That being the case, this useless information can be safely ignored and discarded. The way we ignore this useless information is not by trying to suppress it but by applying one of our distraction techniques from Chapter 4 to displace it.

Related to the "important people are coming" issue is what we sometimes refer to as the "potted palm" phenomenon. This is the increased anxiety some people feel when they have to speak publicly in a more formal setting. "I did okay last week, but that was informal, in the green room. Now I have to give my presentation in the board room," is a complaint we frequently hear.

Sound system issues aside, the furnishings of a particular venue do not add to the physical effort being asked of the speaker. This is simply another cue that a person with stagefright can seize upon to conclude that he is at a greater risk of experiencing personal humiliation. Rather than being intimidated by particular physical surroundings, stagefright-sufferers can displace thoughts about where the presentation will be given by using of the distraction techniques.

LET'S GO AROUND THE ROOM AND INTRODUCE OURSELVES

Some people with stagefright are most sensitized to reading aloud but may find impromptu speaking easier. Others may feel the other way around. Some may find giving a talk from notes most difficult. Either way, everyone with stagefright lives in dread of being at some sort of gathering or function and having someone say, "Let's go around the room and introduce ourselves."

Typically people with stagefright will count and monitor carefully as it comes around to their turn, take a deep breath and try and complete their introduction with a single lung-full of air. This reinforces the thought that they are about to engage in some very dangerous activity, such as bailing out of an airplane, and intensifies the catecholamine release that they experience in other presentation situations. It's also not unheard of after the stagefright-sufferer has done that for someone at back of the room to yell out, "Could you repeat that, we didn't hear you," leaving the poor stagefright-sufferer out of air and out of luck.

There are several universal bad habits that people with stagefright get into during the "let's go around the room and introduce ourselves" situation. It is very instructive to see how many people independently develop the same behaviors in response to the same situation, which brings them to the same stagefright-filled result. This serves as further confirmation of our model of stagefright. At the Stagefright Survival School we teach people to recognize these bad "let's go around the room and introduce ourselves" habits and to avoid falling back on them.

The first of these bad habits is fixating on when your turn is coming. We call this "waiting for the axe to fall." Often the person with stagefright will count and recount when his turn is coming, checking and rechecking whatever pattern is being used to determine who introduces himself or herself next. Of course, while doing this he loses whatever value there was in the whole introduction exercise.

While it is necessary to maintain a degree of alertness so as to be able to respond when appropriate, we teach our students to stop the checking behavior. Instead,

CHAPTER 2: FREQUENT ISSUES IN STAGEFRIGHT

the student is taught that during the "let's go around the room and introduce ourselves" process, she must stay firmly rooted in the present moment, not anticipating when her turn will come. This is done by using the Staying In The Present By Contact With The Physical Environment technique discussed in Chapter 4.

Another bad habit common to people with stagefright in the "going around the room" situation is "rehearsing." This is when you mouth to yourself verbatim what you will say when your turn to talk comes, including your name. This is not quite the same as having the thought that you will mention your new job responsibilities or some other appropriate item.

Typical rehearsing goes like this: "My name is John and I work in...." A persistent belief develops among people with stagefright that there is protective magic attached to saying to yourself exactly what you will say when your turn to introduce yourself comes. Most specifically the belief is that this behavior will save you from going blank. (I will discuss the fear of going blank in more detail later.)

I reassure our students that they know their names and don't need to rehearse them and that they would know them even if telephoned in the middle of the night. Nor is there any protective value to this kind of rehearsal — it merely confirms that you are about to do something you regard as very dangerous but that you will be okay if you can only spit out your introduction in one breath. This kind of thinking is part and parcel of the stagefright thought patterns and further sets you up for a possible panic when your turn actually comes.

Instead of this kind of rehearsal, the person with stagefright who finds himself in the going-around-the-room situation needs to stay at all times in the present moment by use of one of the described techniques. When his turn arrives, he needs to pause momentarily and take command of the situation. Studies have established that the audience views whoever is speaking at that moment as the authority figure.

During that quick pause before speaking, you may apply the "floating" technique where you take a measure of your level of anxiety and allow it to be there. This is particularly important if the participants in the group are standing up to do their introductions. The increased physiological load in going from a seated to a standing position results in an increased heart rate that may be interpreted by the stagefright-sufferer as a rising panic, causing a spiral of anxiety. After pausing and taking command of the situation, our students are taught to compose their introduction as they speak, so that it fully occupies their attention leaving little room for the self-conscious thoughts that cause stagefright.

CHAPTER 2: FREQUENT ISSUES IN STAGEFRIGHT

A third bad habit is "jack-in-the-box" behavior, which means jumping up, if you are supposed to stand, and starting to talk while you are getting out of your seat. This behavior can also occur when, if you are supposed to remain seated, you take a full breath of air and try to get everything out in one breath.

Jack-in-the-box behavior is very compelling to people with stagefright because they would like to be done and on their way home by the time they stand up. Because the mere act of standing increases the physiological load on your heart (which stagefright-sufferers can be very sensitive to), jack-in-the-box can't help, only hurt. Jack-in-the-box behavior creates a mindset that you are about to do something very dangerous like jumping through a fiery hoop, causing your body to react accordingly. Instead, we want people to stand completely, if that is what is being called for, then pause, take command of the situation and let their anxiety level steady up or start to decline before speaking. Then, when they are good and ready they can start to introduce themselves.

Even if the person running the meeting has said, "Let's hurry up and go around the room and introduce ourselves," people with stagefright must take the pause they need to let their anxiety settle down. Stagefright-sufferers are always privileged to take the time they need to apply a distraction technique so they can function properly.

To recap, the three things that people with stagefright must avoid when asked to participate in going-around-the-room-to-introduce-ourselves are: (1) the head count while waiting for the axe to fall (counting how many others there are before your turn comes); (2) rehearsing (muttering to yourself what you are going to say) and (3) jack-in-the-box behavior (jumping up and starting to talk while you are getting out of your seat or trying to spit everything out in one breath).

We remind our students that they may leave something out in an impromptu speaking situation, which is what introducing yourself to a group is. From time to time all speakers leave out something they meant to say when responding extemporaneously without prepared notes. Moreover, no one judges these introductions as they would a presentation; they are supposed to be off the cuff. There is no Pulitzer Prize awarded for the best introduction. The important thing is to manage excess anxiety in this situation by avoiding the bad habits and by applying appropriate techniques to keep yourself in the present moment when faced with this particular exercise.

WHAT DID I SAY?

Although the overwhelming sensation experienced by a stagefright-sufferer is one of relief upon finishing a presentation, some people become anxious because they feel they are not aware of what they have said. "Was I on point or did I end up talking about something entirely irrelevant or inappropriate? I can't remember what I said."

Other presenters who do not actually have stagefright can also experience these thoughts. It is the public speaker's version of post-traumatic stress disorder. This feeling of not knowing what you have said upon concluding your remarks is the normal and natural result of the fact that you can't talk and listen to yourself at the same time. Also, you shouldn't try. If you do, you will tune out the present reality and turn inward, which is a sure recipe for panic.

If you want to listen and comprehend what is being discussed, you must sit down in the audience. If you are presenting, you are participating in a totally different experience from listening and cannot expect to have comprehension in the same way as a listener does.

Although any number of standardized tests may instruct you to read a paragraph and answer questions based on your understanding, none of them ask you to read out loud and then answer questions based on your reading out loud comprehension. Listening and presenting are just too different.

PEOPLE COULD SEE I WAS NERVOUS

Worries about appearing nervous in front of an audience are the thoughts that most commonly trigger stagefright. However, any self-critical associations can set off the stagefright process. The kinds of thoughts that cause the release of your catecholamines typically sound like this: "Wouldn't it be awful if everyone could see how nervous I am?" "Wouldn't it be awful if I made a fool of myself?"

THE NASCAR ASSUMPTION

Because the prospect of giving a presentation excites the would-be presenter who has stagefright, there is an inevitable association made that the presentation is an exciting event for everyone. Of course, on most occasions having to listen to someone give a talk at work or school is the farthest thing from exciting for the people having to listen. The event is often soporific, that is, sleep-inducing, for the audience. Their eyes may glaze over and their lids may become heavy and start to droop. While the figures may vary, it is frequently said that only half, at most, of an audience is paying any attention to the speaker at all, with the remaining percentages off in their own thoughts.

However, the speaker with stagefright has convinced herself that she is about to face a very dangerous situation in which there is great danger of harm from embarrassment so the event becomes invested with the thrill, albeit a negative

CHAPTER 2: FREQUENT ISSUES IN STAGEFRIGHT

one, of an Olympic event for the sufferer. This further intensifies the stagefright process through what may be called "the NASCAR Assumption."

Someone who makes the NASCAR Assumption thinks of the audience as scrutinizing her minutely for the slightest sign of nervousness. It is as if the audience was gathered for the very purpose of seeing a disaster happen, as if they were there to see a thrilling race in which a dramatic car crash might just occur. To use another transportation metaphor, for the person with stagefright, the very purpose of having been asked to give a presentation is to produce the proverbial train wreck with the speaker as the victim-in-chief.

Stagefright-sufferers have very little acceptance of the reality that they have been asked to give a talk because someone thought that certain information had to be transferred from the speaker to the audience. Because the presenter has the sense of being under extreme scrutiny, her feelings of being at risk and in danger are increased, further aggravating the condition.

Audiences are generally sympathetic to the presenter, at least to the extent of the normal civility we extend to strangers. They have not come to witness a train wreck. The only time an audience is made uncomfortable by a presenter's anxiety is in sympathy, when it appears that the presenter is in distress. As a former student wisely taught me: Mostly, it's not about you.

MAGICAL THINKING

People with stagefright are subject to certain kinds of "magical thinking," ideas that have no basis in reality but seem irrefutable to those that have them. Among these is the idea that they will somehow be punished for confidence. This idea may be bolstered by the old aphorism "pride comes before a fall" and the concept of hubris, the classical Greek notion that excessive pride is an offense that will be punished by the gods.

Nothing could be further from the truth. We now know that stagefright is caused by the production of the same catecholamine stimulant chemicals as anyone would produce when in real danger. The stagefright-sufferer is producing these same chemicals in response to the thought of being in social danger of embarrassment. To the extent a person could be genuinely confident, he could not also be afraid of humiliating himself and therefore would not experience stagefright.

Stated slightly differently, you cannot be confident that you will not be harmed by humiliating yourself in front of an audience and at the same time be fearful that you will embarrass yourself. Without that fear, your body will not produce the catecholamines that cause you to appear nervous.

CHAPTER 2: FREQUENT ISSUES IN STAGEFRIGHT

As mentioned earlier, I see the proof of this often in the case of teachers who are completely confident in their classrooms and who do not experience stagefright in what actually may be a challenging situation. However, these teachers may be prone to stagefright when confronting the prospect of Open School or Parent-Teacher Nights when they have to meet with parents. Because they are confident in their classrooms, they will not experience stagefright there. In the latter situation, however, if they feel themselves at risk of embarrassing themselves so they may, in fact, experience stagefright.

In reality, there is no mechanism, cosmic or otherwise, that punishes a person for being confident. There is no scale of justice that tips toward humiliating you just because you were confident. Confidence is free. There is no price to be paid for it, so you should feel free to use it generously.

In the discussion of anticipatory anxiety, I touched upon a closely related kind of magical thinking: the idea that "because I have suffered, worried and lost sleep before presentations in the past and nothing bad happened, I had better repeat that process now." There is simply no connection between any anticipatory discomfort you may have experienced in advance of a presentation and how you feel when the presentation time actually arrives.

Stagefright is caused by the production of catecholamines, alarm chemicals, when you are facing an audience. The alarm chemicals you produced weeks, days or even minutes before your actual presentation are long gone and have nothing to do with it. Any benefit you may feel you achieve by obsessing about your presentation in advance and picturing your discomfort is entirely coincidental, is needless suffering and is a waste of your present moments.

DISTORTED THINKING

While not necessarily "magical" in nature, it is common for people with stagefright to engage in other kinds of thinking that tends to support and continue the stagefright habit. One example of this kind of thinking is viewing a forthcoming presentation as an overwhelming whole.

Anything can be made to seem totally daunting when viewed as a whole instead of as the sum of its individual components. If you took an individual bricklayer and simply said, "I want you to reproduce the Pentagon," he would very likely throw up his hands at the suggestion. On the other hand, if you suggested only that he lay a certain course of bricks, brick by brick according to a specified plan, the suggestion would not seem unreasonable.

Similarly, it is not uncommon for a person with stagefright to focus on the totality of a completed presentation by thinking, "I have to talk for half an hour.

CHAPTER 2: FREQUENT ISSUES IN STAGEFRIGHT

How will I ever be able to do that?" In fact, the half hour will inevitably pass, so the speaker should focus on proceeding from one syllable of a word to the next syllable of the following word, then the one after that and so forth. By learning to focus on an achievable unit, the next syllable of the next word, and not view a presentation as an overwhelming and unmanageable whole, the task becomes less frightening so the speaker's anxiety is reduced.

As we know now, some people with stagefright think of their problem as if it were a disease, like something picked up by unwisely drinking the tap water on a foreign trip. They tend to think of it as a unique disease, something that afflicts only them. Of course, it is highly unlikely that any human malady would affect just one sufferer. If you caught something, it is also likely that many other people are similarly afflicted and have also caught that same disease.

Thinking of stagefright as a disease demoralizes the people who have it by leading them to believe that their condition is beyond their control and may inevitably "flair up" at unpredictable, inconvenient times when they are called upon to give a presentation. The actuality is that stagefright is very much within the control of the person who has it, as episodes are triggered only by thoughts of embarrassment when in front of an audience.

Typically, each person with stagefright tends to think that he is more profoundly affected than other sufferers. I see this manifested in our group program. You might think that a small group of six or fewer people, each of whom has the same problem and shares it with the others, would be a relatively low-anxiety environment for someone with stagefright. For some people, however, our group sessions may be the most challenging environment in which to function, even worse than their work environments. These obsessive people turn the situation around by telling themselves, "Everyone here shares the same problem, wouldn't it be awful if I were the only one who appeared nervous." Of course, such thinking sends the message that they are in heightened danger of humiliating themselves, increasing their fight or flight reactions.

Another common kind of distorted thinking is all or nothing, black or white thinking, which is a manifestation of perfectionism. These people cannot accept the concept that they may be a little nervous and that nervousness is okay. They feel that they must be entirely poised and cool or they have failed completely. The inevitable result of such thinking is to put more chips on the table by telling yourself that you are in greater danger of failure by having someone perceive any small sign of nervousness. This virtually guarantees an unfavorable result.

It is also extremely difficult for people with stagefright to accept that not everything they are experiencing is immediately perceptible to the audience. After all, they are feeling it so the audience must know it. However, just because you feel a physical reaction doesn't mean that everyone sees it. When your heart rate increases or you begin trembling, it isn't necessarily noticeable. Actually, in order for something like tremulousness to become obvious, it must get way worse than the slight tightening of the muscles against each other that you first feel. You are the only one hooked up to your nervous system. The audience is not. We will discuss this further when we consider the Transparency Assumption in Chapter 6.

Studies have shown that there is a direct correlation between the distance from the speaker and the audience's perception of the speaker's nervousness. When researchers ask an audience to rate how nervous they thought a speaker was, those at the front rate the speaker as slightly nervous, those in the middle of the auditorium rate the speaker as less nervous and those in the rear say the presenter was not nervous at all.

Of course people with stagefright can become noticeably uncomfortable, but it's not happening when they first think it is. Because distorted thinking interferes with a stagefright-sufferer's ability to realize he has a margin of safety, he throws the safety margin away by allowing the slightest manifestation of anxiety to increase fear-thinking and to rapidly escalate his anxiety.

PROCRASTINATION

Procrastination can often be a serious problem for people with stagefright. At first glance this may seem somewhat paradoxical since I have repeatedly characterized stagefright-sufferers as obsessive-compulsive perfectionists. However, preparing for a forthcoming presentation represents a commitment to going ahead with it, and that prospect may be too frightening to face. The person with stagefright may simply put off preparing the presentation, daydreaming rather than making meaningful progress and perhaps even missing indicated milestones. Such behavior coming from such a usually dependable employee or student may perplex a stagefright-sufferer's boss or teacher.

As is the case with anticipatory anxiety, the ultimate solution to this sort of procrastination is developing confidence that you can do the presentation when the time comes. In the interim, I suggest that the person with stagefright separate the preparation from the presentation and commit only to meeting the preparation deadlines in a timely manner. If he finds that his thoughts drift off toward picturing the presentation when he should be preparing the material, I suggest that one of the distraction techniques be used such as Staying in the Present by Contact with the Physical Environment or Thought Stoppers.

CHAPTER 2: FREQUENT ISSUES IN STAGEFRIGHT

PREPARATION AND PRESENTATION

When we talked about "going around the room and introducing ourselves," I warned against rehearsing. Remember, however, that rehearsing has a very specific meaning in that context: It means saying silently to yourself what your name is and what you are going to say when it comes your turn to introduce yourself. I do not mean to imply that you should avoid adequately preparing your presentation. There is no substitute for satisfactory preparation. Moreover, the lack of it can detract from any confidence you might otherwise have.

There are several basic formats in which you may be called upon to present. You might be called upon to read something, give a talk from notes or to speak or respond to a topic in an unscripted manner. You need to be able to function in all formats.

For some people, reading aloud is the most difficult and most dreaded manner of presenting, especially if the text is also available to the audience. This is because those people feel it is the most constraining form of public speaking. They feel they must follow the text precisely or they will be easily found out and immediately judged if they make a mistake. These people feel totally trapped. For things that must be presented exactly as written, such as a treasurer's report, for example, or perhaps a portion of a ceremony, reading is the necessary format and cannot be avoided.

Some people find reading aloud the easiest format because they are more worried about presenting in other formats that they think are more self-revealing than reading straight from a text. In either case, it is important to remember that it is virtually impossible to read a page of text without missing a word or making a mistake of some sort. This is because, as discussed earlier, your brain, which recognizes the ink blots on the piece of paper, is a lightening fast electro-chemical computer hooked up to the much slower electro-mechanical apparatus of your vocal chords and tongue with which you pronounce the words. It is almost inevitable that data will be lost in the interface so you will have to learn to accept the fact of making a mistake here and there.

You are much less confined in reading than you might think. You remain in full command of your timing and can use the Slow technique as discussed in Chapter 4 as well as the Emphasis and Inflection technique, also discussed there.

Many — if not most — talks will be given from notes. There are multiple ways to prepare this kind of presentation. One way is to write out the material as if it were going to be read, go over it until you are very familiar with it then reduce your text to sentence fragments that remind you (but do not write it out verbatim) of what you want to say. The refinement can be carried a step

CHAPTER 2: FREQUENT ISSUES IN STAGEFRIGHT

further by reducing the notes to just a few ideas or concepts that remind you of what to cover.

Given enough time you may not even need to refer to notes. Speaking from notes, or without notes if you have enough time to prepare for it, is generally more interesting and engaging than merely reading. The difference between giving a talk from notes versus reading the whole thing is the difference between a homemade and a store-bought cookie.

Each time you give the same presentation from your notes may be a little different from the next but given the advantage of better engaging the audience, it's worth it. If you absolutely cannot depart from your text, you may have to read. Usually, however, when speaking from notes, the fewer the better is the way to go. Some people who give a presentation from notes (or even without them altogether) like to have a full printed copy of their remarks with them and there is nothing wrong with that.

One format that can be extremely problematic for stagefright-sufferers is memorization. It may be unavoidable in some presentation situations such as a musical performance and certainly in the quintessential stagefright experience of reciting lines in a play. Generally, if you're not an actor or student assigned to recite the *Gettysburg Address* to a class or are being inducted into a secret society, you most likely won't be required to memorize. Given a choice, you should always select another format.

Memorization is undesirable because it can put you on automatic pilot and you won't be fully absorbed in your presentation. This can leave a lot of room for the self-conscious thoughts and self-awareness that cause stagefright. If possible, you don't want to memorize your speech or over-practice it to the point that it no longer absorbs your attention when you are presenting.

But what can you do if you are in a play or are assigned to do a recitation? As noted earlier, I've worked with people who suffered from stagefright when giving presentations at work and yet those same people give theatrical performances as a hobby. Nothing required them to adopt this particular hobby and when rehearsing their lines they are completely comfortable. How can that be? There are two answers, each of which tells us how to address a situation in which we must recite from memory.

First, they are fully occupied by the roles they're playing so they are not engaged in the self-conscious awareness that triggers stagefright. If you are in a recitation-from-memory situation that you find does not fully occupy your attention, you will have to use one of your distraction techniques to take your mind off yourself.

CHAPTER 2: FREQUENT ISSUES IN STAGEFRIGHT

The other reason some people with stagefright can also be comfortable acting is that they are in character; they are not themselves. Instead, they are throwing themselves into the role they are portraying. As such they do not feel at risk of personally embarrassing or humiliating themselves and do not activate their fear responses when acting. My advice to anyone who has to recite the *Gettysburg Address* from memory is: When you do it, be Lincoln.

Regardless of the format in which you must present, what if you are not, in fact, well prepared? This can result from procrastination as a part of your stagefright, from some other neglect on your part or without any failure on your part at all. You may be selected to give a particular speech because a knowledgeable presenter is unavailable or because, at that time, you're simply the best the organization can offer.

Not long ago, I worked with a lady who was chosen by her government agency to appear with a local member of Congress to face hostile constituents who were angry over the scope and lack of speed of aid the agency was providing them for a particular program. She knew little about the particulars of the citizens' complaints, nor was it within her job responsibility to do anything about them. Nevertheless, she drew the bureaucratic short straw and was designated to represent the agency on these occasions.

This is hardly unique in presentation situations. Despite your most conscientious efforts you simply may not be up to speed on a particular subject when you are required to present it. You then have two choices. You can dwell on your shortcomings and the likelihood that you will be judged harshly for your presentation, which will not make you any more knowledgeable about your subject but is guaranteed to make you more anxious. Alternatively you can accept that there is nothing you can do at that point about your lack of knowledge or lack of time to prepare, use distraction techniques to clear your mind of self-conscious thinking and at least be less nervous in your delivery.

WHAT DO I TELL THE BOSS?

With the application of the principles in this book this question should become more and more unnecessary. However, we frequently see people who haven't addressed their stagefright until brought to a crisis, usually by being assigned to give a presentation they can't easily avoid. Not infrequently, I have been asked the question, "What do I tell the boss?" When this happens I have to explain that although we have unraveled the cognitive patterns of stagefright and scientists have discovered the chemical pathways through which it operates, "What do I tell the boss?" is, and must remain, a question beyond the reach of scientists or philosophers.

Based on the empirical evidence that has been gathered when people have had to tell their bosses that they suffer from stagefright, the range of responses runs the familiar bell-shaped curve. Starting on the one side, we have, "Oh, my God, you have stagefright, too, who are we going to send now?" Further along the continuum we have, "Since there is still time, let's get you some help." Somewhere in the middle we have, "Well, go over your material carefully and be sure to practice and you'll be fine." Finally at the other end of the spectrum we have, "This job requires you to be able to communicate effectively."

As you can see, the response may range from the sympathetic and even empathetic all the way to the angered and annoyed. Most responses will probably fall somewhere in the middle. This actually presents a problem. Because some degree of nervousness in giving a presentation is normal and universal, many people just don't understand the kind of extreme stagefright that would lead someone to have this sort of conversation with a supervisor in the first place.

If your boss may have gotten a little nervous herself but is always ultimately fine, she may not understand the kind of profound physical reactions — the racing heart, hyperventilation, trembling, sweating and loss of sleep for days or longer — that may lead a stagefright-sufferer to avoid speaking before an audience. The best answer, therefore, has to be to apply the principles you are learning so you don't have to have that particular conversation.

PERFECTIONISM

We have previously discussed perfectionism and identified it as the backbone upon which stagefright is built and described how it raises the stakes of the game because perfectionists are unwilling to appear even a little nervous. They fear showing their nervousness, thereby ratcheting up the normal level of anxiety that is present in facing an audience. Thus, perfectionist people magnify the problem because they are extremely intolerant to their own nervousness. But who wants to be less than perfect?

The core disadvantage of perfectionism can be found in the maxim "the perfect is the enemy of the good." There is nothing inherently wrong in striving for a good outcome or product. But the only way to be perfect is not to make a mistake. The only way not to make a mistake is to do nothing. This is the kind of paralysis perfectionism leads to when followed in an uncritical way. If we are willing to experience the almost inevitable mistakes — including appearing to be nervous — then we lift a tremendous self-imposed burden from our shoulders and are more likely to have a better, more productive result.

CHAPTER 2: FREQUENT ISSUES IN STAGEFRIGHT

NONVERBAL PRESENTATIONS

I said in Chapter 1 that stagefright was equally applicable to nonverbal presentations, such as a demonstration of some sort, even if the presenter doesn't have to say a word. I have used the term "stagefright" throughout because most people understand what that means. A better, more descriptive term would be "performance anxiety" to refer to any time a person feels that she is the subject of the attention of others.

Subscribe to a Google alert on the word "stagefright" and the overwhelming number of references you will receive have to do with sports. Stagefright apparently has become a regular staple in sportswriters' lexicons. They use it to describe everything that has to do with a substandard or disappointing performance in the world of sports. It can be used to refer to poor coordination on the part of a team. It can be poor planning, tactics and execution by a team or an individual athlete. It can be bad or inexperienced coaching.

Of course, none of those things has anything to do with real stagefright. In sports, stagefright really only applies to those circumstances in which an individual athlete, to borrow from the sportswriter's lexicon, "chokes." The behavior to which that term applies is indeed stagefright because it represents the same self-poisoning with one's own catecholamines that I have been describing. If a person who is about to make a golf shot or perform some other athletic task turns his attention inward, even momentarily, and has the thought or association that he will fail or possibly embarrass himself, the immediate physiological reaction is one of being in danger which prompts the body to respond in the only way it can when it perceives danger: by releasing catecholamines. The effects of catecholamines under those circumstances are equally as deleterious as they are when you are trying to give a talk.

You will recall that one of the effects we discussed was that catecholamines caused opposing muscles to contract against each other, causing trembling. This effect is particularly important in sports because it alters a person's kinesthetic sense, that is, the brain's understanding of where the various body parts, arms, legs, hands, are and what it takes to move them. Now, instead of an athlete's body feeling as it did during practice when she tried to make a particular shot in golf or basketball or carry out some other athletic maneuver, her body is "handling" very differently. It's as if she were wearing weights, which is more than enough to throw her off and actually cause her to miss an otherwise frequently successful shot.

A former colleague described a tableau he observed from his backyard that illustrates the point. There was a piece of ground with a depression in it where

CHAPTER 2: FREQUENT ISSUES IN STAGEFRIGHT

children would play. Someone had placed a plank of wood over the depression and the children liked to practice balancing on it as they walked across.

Most of the time the children had little difficulty in negotiating the board. However, after it rained, the depression filled with water and the board then spanned a big mud puddle instead of dry ground. He noticed that on those occasions, the children became much shakier in their balance beam performances and more likely to fall off.

He hypothesized that under dry conditions, with little at stake, the children were relaxed and more easily able to cross the board. However, when the board spanned a mud puddle and the consequences of falling off would be getting muddy and having to face their moms, the children's kinesthetic senses were thrown off, making it more likely that they would fall.

Even if a public appearance is entirely nonverbal, the same stagefright principles apply. As with speaking before a group, you need to apply a distraction technique to clear your mind of self-critical thoughts so you don't produce the catecholamines that can disrupt your performance. If anyone should ask you, "Will reading this book improve my golf game?" my suggested answer is: "Couldn't hurt!"

CHAPTER 3
MANAGING STAGEFRIGHT

The fundamental principle in managing stagefright is easy to state. In fact, it can be set forth in a single, simple declarative sentence — but it is not the least bit easy to apply. It takes a clear understanding of the mechanisms of stagefright, the cognitive pattern that initiates it, the body's reaction to those thoughts and a lot of practice and training in distraction techniques to short circuit the stagefright process.

Essentially, the fundamental principle for managing stagefright follows the fundamental principle of tightrope walking – don't look down. Adapted to stagefright it is this: **When you are talking to an audience of one or more people, don't think about yourself.**

Our model of the process of stagefright has been confirmed to us hundreds of times over more than two decades of practical experience. When, having just met someone, I can describe the thought process by which he initiates his stagefright and have him recognize and identify it, we know we are right on target. Therefore, the first step in managing stagefright is to have a thorough understanding of what is actually taking place. Next comes applying that understanding to altering that process.

The difficulty in applying the "don't think about yourself" principle occurs from the very start. You can't stop thinking about yourself by suppressing that thought. It doesn't work. Trying to suppress self-conscious thoughts encompasses within it the very thought you are trying to suppress. Moreover, if you tell an obsessive-compulsive sort of person that they must not think about a purple elephant, he is going to immediately have the most magnificent, vivid image of a purple elephant imaginable.

You cannot suppress a thought by struggling against it since that just makes it more compelling. Putting it in martial arts terms, you cannot box or wrestle against an unwanted thought. Any force you apply simply rebounds back at you. Instead of boxing or wrestling against it, we have to apply judo and let it throw itself over of its own weight. In other words, the way to get rid of an unwanted thought is by displacing it with another thought, which is why we employ distraction techniques. Applying these techniques interrupts your self-conscious thoughts so your body does not react as if you are in danger. The way to get rid of an unwanted thought is not by trying to suppress it but rather by distracting yourself from having it.

Managing stagefright consists of practicing the distraction techniques and, whenever possible, using a "prompting," a written word or phrase to remind us to use the technique so we can displace any fear-thoughts that may arise during a presentation. Because the catecholamine chemicals that are responsible for our fight or flight responses are destroyed rather rapidly on production, if we can stop the thinking that triggers their release as soon as we become aware of getting anxious, we can halt the stagefright process before it becomes noticeable and gets out of hand.

In Chapter 7 I describe some medications that can help manage stagefright. The medications are integrated with the distraction techniques: They act on the release of catecholamines that initiate the fight or flight response. The distraction techniques are designed to displace the triggering fear-thoughts that cause you to produce the catecholamines in the first place, reducing or perhaps even eliminating catecholamine release. The medications reduce production of catecholamines or block their effects altogether. As described in more detail in Chapter 7, beta blockers work by competitively occupying the receptor sites to which the catecholamines molecules need to attach to have their effect, which makes thoughts of embarrassing yourself less compelling.

The relative roles of distraction techniques and medication can be compared to the analogy of having water in your basement from a leaky pipe. In the case of stagefright, we are dealing not with water but with catecholamines. If you want to optimally regain use of that wet basement, you need to do two things: First you must tighten down the valve or patch the pipe that is responsible for the leak. That is the equivalent of what we are doing when we apply the distraction techniques to reduce the fear-thinking that results in the release of catecholamines. Then you need to mop and bail the basement, which is how the medications function in this instance.

You can use the distraction techniques by themselves because by stopping the fear-thoughts that cause the catecholamine release, you reduce or eliminate your nervousness, which results in a more poised presentation. Some people choose to do just this. What you can't do is only use medication without the distraction techniques because the medications don't work as well without the help of the distractions. If you don't manage your thinking so that you displace the self-conscious thoughts, your body will continue to produce catecholamines to get you ready to face danger. You can potentially reach a point where you will over-flood the level of protection provided by the medication because your body is a more efficient pharmaceutical factory than any of the ones built by the medication manufacturers.

Over the years I have worked with any number of people who have tried beta blockers, sometimes at dosages significantly more than ordinarily used for stagefright, and felt they did little if any good. On the other hand, once they understood the mechanisms of stagefright and the need to displace the self-

CHAPTER 3: MANAGING STAGEFRIGHT

conscious thoughts and were equipped with distraction techniques, they found the addition of the beta blocker very helpful.

Another important aspect of managing stagefright is forgiving yourself if you are convinced that people in your audience could tell you were nervous or panicky. When I suggest this to people with stagefright, the typical reaction is one of disgust and dismissal. "I don't want to appear nervous and I don't see why I should forgive myself if it happens," someone may respond. After all, if she was visibly nervous before an audience, the worst thing, a totally unacceptable thing, how could she possibly forgive herself? She feels like she doesn't deserve to forgive herself.

I am not patting you on the back and saying, "There, there, it's okay to forgive yourself." Nor am I being comforting and saying nobody probably noticed, which might or might not be true. Not at all. I am saying you must forgive yourself. Forgiveness is mandatory and essential in order to manage stagefright.

You have no choice but to forgive yourself. What is done is done and cannot be undone. Life is not a videotape that can be rewound and re-recorded over. Next, and more important, not forgiving yourself supports and intensifies the very stagefright you are trying to overcome. The pain, suffering and mental self-flagellation most stagefright-suffers undergo following a panicky experience actually feeds the stagefright.

Remember, the typical central thought that initiates stagefright is that you may appear nervous when giving a presentation. By punishing yourself with critical thoughts after a panicky episode, you are raising the stakes, putting more chips on the table for next time. If you feared appearing nervous in front of an audience before, think of how much more you will fear it after having punished yourself following that occasion. The thinking typically becomes: "You better not mess up this time. Remember how bad you felt last time?"

Berating yourself following an unsatisfactory performance accomplishes nothing positive. If it did, stagefright would be an immediately self-correcting process. Punishing yourself for having appeared nervous does one thing and one thing only and that is to set you up for a worse outcome next time.

The ideas of forgiveness and acceptance become especially important with respect to the notion of setbacks. You have had one or more successful, low-anxiety performances followed by one that was not satisfactory to you. Under these circumstances, some people feel that they have had a setback and that the progress they have made has been taken away from them. Such an experience can be extremely frustrating, demoralizing and even lead to depression.

CHAPTER 3: MANAGING STAGEFRIGHT

There is actually no such thing as a setback. Each time you do a presentation is a new, separate experience. On a particular occasion you may forget or disregard the things you have learned and return to the thinking pattern that causes you to invoke your body's chemical fear responses. Or you can apply the things you have learned, use your distraction techniques to clear your mind of fear-thoughts and experience less anxiety. Each presentation is new and each time it's up to you to manage your stagefright.

Nor can anything be taken away from you. You won't forget the things you have learned. Nobody can take away your new knowledge about how to deal with stagefright. The only thing that can possibly happen is that on a particular occasion you fail to apply the things you know.

After I'd been driving for many, many years, one day I backed my car out of my garage while fiddling with the radio and ripped the molding from around the garage door. That doesn't mean I need to retake driving lessons. It means that on that particular occasion I simply wasn't paying attention to what I was doing. Applying distraction techniques is like that. The only way you can defeat them is by not applying them on a particular occasion. Once you learn them, you will always have them.

Sometimes a series of successful, low-anxiety presentations can actually become an excuse for a new anxiety. This is the fear of having a setback and spoiling your growing good record. This is just old fear-thinking in a new wrapper. Fear of spoiling a series of successes is just fear of embarrassing yourself, which is stagefright. You deal with it by managing your stagefright by applying your distraction techniques during each separate presentation. A successful series is built one event at a time. It is, in one special sense, like flipping a coin. You still have a 50 percent chance of getting heads on any one toss even if the coin has landed on heads 100 consecutive times already.

In the case of flipping coins, over the long run you will still get heads 50 percent of the time. But if you apply your techniques consistently you will get good results consistently and build your confidence as well. If you fail to apply your techniques, there is always the possibility that the result may come up tails when you wanted heads. The difference, of course, is that unlike flipping a coin, your anxiety in giving a presentation is not in any way dependent on chance. It is wholly dependent on your managing your stagefright by using your techniques to stop thinking about your self.

The next presentation is not, except in one important respect, dependent on the previous one. That exception is that as you go along you can build confidence. But, whether you are confident or not, if you apply your distraction techniques to clear your self-critical thoughts, you will have a successful experience.

CHAPTER 3: MANAGING STAGEFRIGHT

It is also very helpful for people with stagefright to gain some realistic perspective of how they appear to others. As unpalatable as this may sound to someone with stagefright, the only real way this can be achieved is by being videotaped. When positive feedback is received in a group setting, the stagefright-sufferer invariably dismisses it. The typical thought is, "It's very nice of them to say I didn't look nervous but they're such terrible liars."

As we discussed when I talked about distorted thinking, the reason that stagefright-sufferers are so convinced they are not being given an honest appraisal is because they know what they experienced by way of feelings and physical reactions. No amount of supportive reassurance is going to convince them that even if they felt nervous they didn't show it. Because the sensations the stagefright-sufferer experienced were 100 percent real, it is very hard to accept any feedback that discounts how he felt when interpreting what others may have perceived. Because he felt an increase in heart rate, a disruption in breathing rhythm and, perhaps, visible trembling, it is very hard to convince that person that others did not experience or recognize his anxiety in the same way. This is discussed further as the "transparency issue."

People with stagefright have a far greater margin of safety than they may ever have thought. That is not to say that people with stagefright never get noticeably distressed in front of an audience. That can certainly happen. But it does not happen when the person with stagefright first thinks it is happening. The reason for that is that the stagefright-sufferer is the only one actually stuffed into her own skin. She may feel opposing muscles begin to contract against each other but that process must proceed quite a bit before that physiology becomes noticeable to an audience as trembling.

The presenter will feel when her heart rate picks up or breathing becomes disrupted but it is also highly unlikely that an audience member can notice that her heart rate has increased or that her breathing rhythm has altered until these reactions have progressed significantly — or until the presenter has become distracted by them. The only way most people with stagefright can come to accept that they have this margin of safety is by watching themselves on videotape, disconnected from their own nervous systems.

It is also quite amazing to see the wide range of apparent or discernable anxiety in proclaimed stagefright-sufferers. Some people, not surprisingly, may show some overt signs of anxiety. What is surprising, however, is the number of people who exhibit no obvious nervousness whatsoever yet who are so troubled by their stagefright that they are willing to commit their time and resources to overcome it.

There is nothing about managing stagefright that is in the least bit passive. It is not like going to the dentist and having a cavity filled or like taking your car

CHAPTER 3: MANAGING STAGEFRIGHT

to the body shop, having a dent hammered out and picking it up after lunch. Stagefright can't be overcome by just reading this book or even by taking our course. It can only be overcome by individual people learning and applying the principles for overcoming stagefright in their own bodies.

Stagefright is caused by the release of catecholamines in response to thoughts or awareness that you are in danger of embarrassing yourself. It can only be mediated by understanding the mechanism and applying the distraction techniques we discuss in this book to clear your mind of the triggering thoughts so you don't produce the chemicals that cause the racing heart, disrupted breathing rhythm and tremulousness that is stagefright.

A person with stagefright should approach each presentation with the mindset that it will never end. The time, of course, will pass and at some point the presentation will be over. But in approaching the presentation and while giving it, the presenter should adopt the perspective that she will be there giving the presentation forever.

At first this may sound like it would make your stagefright worse but once this approach is adopted, the prospect of escape is removed and the state of fight or flight becomes harder to sustain. Any thought of fleeing, no matter how unlikely it is for you to actually run off, is likely to keep up the production of catecholamines and your body's state of alarm. If you can eliminate all daydreams that leaving soon is possible, you will begin to wind down the fight or flight responses, which have now become of no value to you. Remember, the time will take care of itself as it always does, you can't stop it, but equally, you can't rush it.

As stated earlier, stagefright tends to be an ongoing problem. This is not because of some relapse or recurrence like a disease but simply because on any given occasion a person with stagefright may fail to apply the things he has learned. As soon as a stagefright-sufferer engages, however briefly, in self-conscious thoughts, he will be flooded with his body's fight or flight chemicals.

Because of this, it is helpful for people with stagefright to think of themselves somewhat in the same way that people with an alcohol problem think about themselves. They have a potentially recurring problem that must be addressed by applying the techniques they have learned for dealing with it and avoiding prior bad habits. As we have already observed, it is also useful to recognize that because of its continuing nature, it is better to think in terms of overcoming or managing stagefright rather than "curing" it.

At some point, if you practice and apply these principles, you may start to have comfortable presentations. At this point, the anxiety of stagefright may appear

CHAPTER 3: MANAGING STAGEFRIGHT

strangely absent. When this happens it is important not to go looking for those fearful feelings because if you do, you will find them. Again, there is no magic to this, it's all atoms and gears and wheels and molecules. If you entertain thoughts along the lines of, "I don't feel anxious, I wonder what happened," you are effectively invoking the fear-thoughts and will release the catecholamines that cause your stagefright.

CHAPTER 4
DISTRACTION TECHNIQUES FOR OVERCOMING STAGEFRIGHT

> *"Stage fright is something a lot of people experience. It's fear of being judged by someone else. I think that comes by way — very specifically — of putting your attention on yourself. If you put your attention outside of yourself, on the subject or person or something other than you, then stage fright goes away."* Wayne Rogers, actor

> *"I have faith in the power of distraction."* Woody Allen, director, writer, actor

Fear-thoughts in a public speaking situation produce physiological changes that can be disabling. The cycle goes like this: you have fear-thoughts, your body releases chemicals that initiate physiological reactions; these reactions reinforce the original thoughts and this reinforcement produces yet greater physiological reactions that may result in incapacitation. The logical place to break the cycle, therefore, is with the thoughts. If you can stop fear-thoughts, there will be no physiological reactions that will interfere with, or detract from, your performance.

The question then is, how do we achieve this? If you say to someone, "Well, just don't think about that, don't think about getting nervous in front of the audience," that is not very helpful. Particularly when dealing with the obsessive-compulsive person, such a suggestion will only produce more anxiety because the individual, in addition to her other phobic thinking, is now anxious about her inability to stop having the unwanted fear-thoughts.

The more someone is told not to have that thought, the more difficult she may find it to rid herself of precisely that thought. In the first place, trying not to think about something means by definition that you have to acknowledge the thought that you're trying to suppress. In the second place, trying not to think about something, particularly for someone with a stagefright-prone personality, may lead to an almost irresistible impulse to concentrate on exactly the thought that is supposed to be suppressed. As we have observed, it's kind of like poking your new dental work with your tongue.

The techniques that follow will enable you to rid yourself of your unwanted thoughts. Naturally, some people will be more comfortable with some of these techniques than with others. A variety is provided so you can pick the things that work best for you and also because they have different purposes.

CHAPTER 4: DISTRACTION TECHNIQUES FOR OVERCOMING STAGEFRIGHT

These techniques have the following in common: They are ways of *distracting yourself* from thinking about yourself without, of course, being so compelling as to distract you from your presentation. They are designed to act like "shoe horns" to seamlessly move your attention away from yourself back to the subject matter of your presentation.

Stagefright comes from exaggerated self-consciousness. To be more relaxed, you must lose that excessive self-awareness. We do this by distracting ourselves from thinking about ourselves. Remember, **the only way to rid yourself of an unwelcome thought is not by trying not to have that thought but by learning how to displace it.**

You will notice that not all techniques have the same application. Some are useful before a presentation, some during and some even after. We are collecting them all together here to provide you with a toolbox from which you can select the right technique for your particular needs, much as you would chose a hammer to drive a nail but a screwdriver to drive a screw.

There are some important points to address. First, **you should not pick more than one technique for use during your presentation.** The reason you should stick with one technique is because we use prompts to remind you to use that technique. If you pick more than one, you are likely to flit back and forth between them and end up using neither technique.

Second, **techniques always work and cannot be defeated.** The only way to "defeat" a technique and appear to have it fail is by not using it. This is because no one can think about three things at once. You can be thinking about yourself and struggling through your presentation but you can't be giving your presentation, paying attention to yourself and be applying a technique to clear your mind of fear-thoughts all at the same time. No one can multitask that well.

Applying a technique with adequate concentration will quickly clear your mind of thinking about yourself so that your attention becomes fully occupied with your presentation, which is where you want it to be. When you stop thinking about your vulnerability to embarrassment, you will cease the catecholamine release that results in the physical discomfort of stagefright.

Walter Mischel, a social psychology professor from Columbia University, has provided a useful metaphor and vocabulary that can be used to characterize stagefright and how we can manipulate it. He describes a "hot system" he characterizes as, "an emotional system, a reflexive system, an automatic system, a system that is much closer to the unconscious. It's automatic and it's essentially the natural default."

CHAPTER 4: DISTRACTION TECHNIQUES FOR OVERCOMING STAGEFRIGHT

Mischel's hot system correlates to what we have been referring to as the fight or flight reaction that initiates the chemical cascade (the "self-poisoning with one's own catecholamines") that follows from a thought of being in danger of embarrassing or humiliating yourself. This hot system, Mischel suggests, probably resides largely in the amygdala and ventral striatum in the brain, is there from birth and is tremendously accentuated by stress so it goes up exactly when we need it most — when we're in truly dangerous situations. The exception, of course, is that it is precisely the activation of this hot system that we don't want people to see when we are in front of an audience.

Mischel's "cool system," by contrast, takes place much more in the prefrontal cortex, which is involved in higher intellectual functions. He describes it as cognitive, slower, more complex and reflective rather than reflexive.

When we apply a distraction technique, we are engaging the cool system of higher cognitive functions to govern and overrule the faster, automatic, reflexive and emotional hot system. This is not easy but it is doable and this is the only way to manage stagefright without outside assistance.

PROMPTING

Regardless of the technique being employed, it will be necessary for you to have some "prompting," some message or other reminder to employ the technique. No matter how comfortable you may feel with a particular technique in practice, it is always possible for self-conscious fear-thinking to return.

After all, if you had the presence of mind to call upon a technique in the middle of a presentation, without some reminder, you probably would not have stagefright in the first place.

The prompting should be clear and convenient, some word or short message written on your notes or other material that immediately calls to mind the specific technique you plan to employ. When the spiraling fear starts, there is no time to fumble for a reminder. The prompt should be visible so that the technique can be applied as soon as fear-thought presents themselves. It is best to work with one technique at a time. Prompting for more than one technique can get confusing so that it no longer triggers the right response.

STAYING IN THE PRESENT BY CONTACT WITH THE PHYSICAL ENVIRONMENT

Phobic future-thinking is the term used to describe what happens when you start imagining "What if..." or "How do I know..." One way to displace an unwanted phobic future-thought is by staying in the present by returning your thoughts to

CHAPTER 4: DISTRACTION TECHNIQUES FOR OVERCOMING STAGEFRIGHT

the present reality as opposed to the negative imaginary future that your brain can conjure up. This is effective with almost any kind of anxiety that is based on future-thinking.

One way to root your thinking firmly in the present is by contact with the reality of the physical environment. For example, try to concentrate on the surface of an object in front of you. It can be a table, chair, sofa or a lectern. Concentrate on its surface. Try to commit to memory every aspect of its texture, grain and color variations. If you have concentrated fully, you will realize that for that portion of a second, you were aware of nothing else and that any anxiety you may have had was lessened.

This exercise can be done using any of the senses, especially sight, hearing or touch, to open what we might think of as the external cognitive pathway for information coming in from outside. At the same time, this closes what we might call the internal cognitive pathway used in generating fear-thoughts. Once you can break the cycle of fear-thinking for even the tiniest portion of a second, you can prevent the spiraling that leads to incapacitating panic.

Disabling panic does not arise spontaneously in the case of stagefright. It is the final step in the stagefright continuum. Think of this kind of panic as number 10 on a progression of fear starting from 0, which is the total absence of anxiety. Spiraling through the stagefright process may progress very rapidly so a person may feel that her panic arises spontaneously. In reality, at the moment the fear-thinking starts, she is not actually suffering a disabling panic.

The public speaking situation offers many opportunities to return to the present. This can be done by concentrating on a lectern or conference table in front of you, getting in contact with the feeling of the rug or flooring under your feet, by concentrating on the feel and texture of the paper containing your notes or text or by focusing on someone in the audience, trying to see the weave of their clothing or pores of their skin.

In all instances, it is important that contact be made with the environment with full concentration. There is no help in looking at or rubbing away at a lectern without genuinely applying your concentration to get in touch with the physical environment. It is your full mental concentration that is important so any touching motion cannot become mechanical.

It takes at most only a few seconds to break the train of your fear-thinking and get your attention focused on your presentation rather than yourself. At that point, your levels of anxiety will be way down. Basically, human beings are capable of one thought at a time. A person with stagefright, however, is really trying to do two things at the same time. On the one hand, she is trying to give

CHAPTER 4: DISTRACTION TECHNIQUES FOR OVERCOMING STAGEFRIGHT

a talk. At the same time she is really engaged in fear-thinking: "How do I know I can get through it, what if I have to leave, how do I know I won't get panicky," and even, "What if I'm boring, how do I know the audience will like me," and so forth. By soaking up the intellectual capacity used in this fear-thinking, reorienting it to the present moment of the presentation, the consequence of the fear-thinking can be avoided and a more effective speech is given. Contact with the physical environment achieves this but only when it is applied with true concentration.

OUTWARD FOCUS

Outward Focus is perhaps the most straightforward and direct of the techniques. When you look at your prompt, the written word or phrase to remind you to apply your chosen technique, and see "Outward Focus," it will remind you to stop thinking about yourself and to redirect your full attention back to your presentation.

SLOWING DOWN

One of the most important techniques for the anxious speaker is slowing down. Most, but not all, anxious speakers speak too rapidly. It is not unlike attempting to flee a truly dangerous situation. The behavioral maxim is "I run, therefore I fear." It is not uncommon for someone with stagefright to begin speaking from his seat, even before reaching the place in the room from which the presentation is to be given. This is an attempt to outrun the feared situation to "white knuckle it" and get through the speech, preferably in one breath, before the danger catches up. This, of course, is impossible since you cannot outrun your own fear. Instead, haste actually intensifies the fear reaction. Even for speakers who don't talk noticeably fast, the slowing down technique is important.

When facing what would otherwise be a disabling level of anxiety, by speaking slowly, one syllable at a time, your presentation can go on. If you speak that slowly, even under the burden of an intense fear reaction that brings on rapid shallow breathing, you will not begin hyperventilating and be unable to talk. There are other benefits as well. Speaking slowly comes across as thoughtful, deliberate and collected to the audience.

Knowing that when you become anxious you will employ this technique and still be able to go on with your presentation provides you with the reassurance that you have probably sought all along. You may even come to think of it as building a protective cocoon of slowing down to which you may retreat whenever you like.

The discipline of the slower-than-natural cadence, like contact with the physical environment, absorbs the excess intellectual energy used to engage in fear-

CHAPTER 4: DISTRACTION TECHNIQUES FOR OVERCOMING STAGEFRIGHT

thinking. It is possible for you to be engaged in fear-thinking and stumble through a presentation with fear. It is not possible for you to speak more slowly than you normally would, deliver your talk and also be engaged in fear-thinking. No one can divide her attention in three parts. Finally, the slow cadence sends a message of comfort, safety and relaxation throughout the body that soon causes a reversal of the physiological fear reactions.

As with any of the techniques, you will not be actually doing it for a full minute or even 30 seconds. It takes only a few seconds to distract yourself from thinking about your fears. At that point, your full attention will be directed to your presentation and your fight or flight reactions will subside.

A good exercise is to read aloud a passage from a book or magazine and time your reading. Then reread it aloud making your reading last about 1½ times as long. Slowing down and doing this reading exercise must be accomplished smoothly and uniformly to achieve the desired results. Simply pausing between bursts of speech is not slowing down and will not have a beneficial effect.

TAKING THINGS SYLLABLE BY SYLLABLE

As in the case of other phobias, the stagefright-sufferer tends to think of the task to be done as an overwhelming, indivisible whole. Seeing the totality of the presentation leads to a helpless trapped feeling. This technique focuses on getting the anxious speaker to realize that even a marathon Fidel Castro–style 6-hour speech is only made up of syllables. It is the syllables that are the basic units of the presentation, and every talk is presented one syllable at a time.

You can come to see a big presentation as manageable by breaking down a paragraph into syllables and presenting it to a practice group. As with all techniques, when the actual speaking situation arrives it is necessary to have some prompting device that will remind you to focus back on the manageable syllables and away from the overwhelming whole of the presentation. This is particularly true of those points in the presentation at which you think thoughts of being trapped may arise.

EMPHASIS AND INFLECTION

As we have demonstrated, anxiety in public speaking is involved when you attempt to do two things at once: At the same time you are attempting to give your presentation, you are also involved in self-conscious awareness of potential embarrassment. Thus, anything that can be done to absorb the intellectual capacity with which you are entertaining those fear-thoughts and self-awareness will lead to diminished anxiety. One of the techniques that can help is to focus on providing greater emphasis and interpretation.

CHAPTER 4: DISTRACTION TECHNIQUES FOR OVERCOMING STAGEFRIGHT

Like a piece of music, a talk is really just the skeleton of what the listener hears. Just as a musician can take the same notes and provide very different interpretations, so can a speaker take a single sentence and provide a wide range of interpretations.

Take, for example, the simple opening "Good Morning, I am very glad to be here with you today." This can be rendered as, "Good Morning, I am *very glad* to be here with you today." Or: "Good Morning, I am very glad to be here *with you* today," or "Good Morning, I am very glad to be here with you *today*," among other possible variations.

When the intellectual capacity being used for the fear-thinking is diverted toward providing emphasis to the particular presentation, it not only reduces anxiety but leads to a more effective presentation. This is one example of the several ways in which those skills that reduce anxiety also result in a better public speaking performance.

An exercise that is useful here is to take a paragraph and see how many different ways you can interpret it, how many different emphases and variations it can be given. Again, as with all techniques, you will need to use prompts written on your notes to remind yourself to speak with creative emphasis when your fear-thoughts rear up.

WANTING TO BE THERE

People with stagefright share some feelings with people who have other phobias, particularly claustrophobia. In particular they share the feeling of being trapped. In actuality, in order to be truly trapped, two things must occur. First, there must be constraint. Second, the desire to leave has to be present.

The constraint here can be the physical constraint that troubles the claustrophobic when in a confined space, or it can be a social constraint where you feel you just can't leave. When giving a talk, you are obviously not physically constrained but you may feel the social constraint of not being able to leave, not being able to walk out on your audience.

To be truly confined, you must also want to leave. If you were confined in a room but had no desire to leave and were provided with everything that you need, you would not experience phobic anxiety. The key element here is the desire to leave. This is what troubles a claustrophobic. As soon as she is faced with some measure of physical constraint, she begins to test herself with the desire to leave. There may be no real reason to want to leave the situation, but the claustrophobic thinks, "How can I get out," "What if I have to get out," which soon leads to "I can't get out."

CHAPTER 4: DISTRACTION TECHNIQUES FOR OVERCOMING STAGEFRIGHT

In the case of stagefright, by and large you are in the situation because you put yourself there and you actually want to be there or you want to be able to engage in public speaking. Thus, you can sometimes relieve the anxiety that stems from the feeling of being trapped by a note or other prompting device to remind you that you are not trapped because you really want to be there.

THOUGHT STOPPERS

One of the most troubling areas to many stagefright-sufferers is long-term fearful anticipation, which can make your life miserable weeks, or even months, in advance of your presentation. Over and over again you may run through the future event in your mind picturing and rehearsing every detail, how the room will look and what will happen.

The first principle here is to separate the real from the imaginary. If you truly believe that you can foresee the future or that a high level of anxiety and suffering before the event will somehow ensure a better performance, then perhaps you should be allowed to persist in your discomfort. If, on the other hand, you recognize that you are only making yourself uncomfortable and in no way altering the ultimate outcome, there is help.

You must remember what you intellectually know, which is that you cannot foretell the future and cannot alter the outcome by trying to picture it. Otherwise you might as well panic every time you perform since you are already experiencing that suffering. Whenever you begin to picture future speaking events, picture seeing the room through the doorway of a bank vault, then slam the vault door closed and turn the wheel. Immediately afterwards go do something useful in the present, no matter how trivial the task may be.

Another thought stopper technique involves placing a rubber band around your wrist (make sure it is not too tight to impede circulation). Every time you become aware of engaging in anticipatory thinking of a future speaking event, snap the rubber band and remind yourself that you are not speaking now. Then remind yourself of some constructive activity that needs to be accomplished and immediately take a step associated with that activity.

Anticipatory anxiety is a reinforced habit with some of the characteristics of addictive behavior. In particular, it feeds on a need for control that many people with stagefright seem to feel.

Another technique to help manage anticipatory anxiety is to keep a log of your long-term anticipatory thinking. Note what you were doing and thinking about immediately before you started picturing an upcoming talk. Other items to be noted are the time and duration of anticipatory thoughts. Keeping such a log will start to extinguish the anticipatory anxiety habit.

CHAPTER 4: DISTRACTION TECHNIQUES FOR OVERCOMING STAGEFRIGHT

FLOATING

A large measure of stagefright arises from the struggle to maintain control in the face of our own emergency responses. If, however, instead of fighting for control and trying to force the anxiety away, you simply allow it to be there, the process ceases and the anxiety will diminish. This is one of several ways of achieving what the late Australian psychiatrist Dr. Claire Weekes called "floating."

As discussed under "Wanting to be There," stagefright is closely related to claustrophobia. In fact, stagefright may be thought of as the social equivalent of claustrophobia. A claustrophobic person experiences anxiety together with the fight or flight response when she is physically confined. The person with stagefright experiences the same reaction when he is socially confined. That is, the person with stagefright believes that he cannot walk out during a presentation. Typically, when claustrophic people are instructed to remain seated in a chair for a designated time period, they might think, "How do I know I can stay here? Wouldn't it be awful if I had to leave?" and may experience the racing heart, hyperventilation and tight muscles familiar to anyone with stagefright. They are engaged in a struggle to stay in the chair but who are they struggling against? The answer, of course, is themselves.

Floating, in this context, means recognizing that you are struggling and then letting go of the struggle. To an extent, we practice what can be called the Henny Youngman school of medicine. Raising his hand in the air, Youngman, a comedian and legendary master of the one-liner, tells us, "I went to the doctor. I told him it hurts when I do this. He told me, 'Don't do this.'"

There are at least two ways of learning how to float. The first involves becoming a student of your own anxiety levels. Take a measure of your level of apprehension and put a number on it on a scale of 0 to 10. A 0 would be a complete absence of anxiety, and a 10 would be a complete panic. A panic means that you are aware only of your own panic and you don't even know where you are at the moment.

Floating requires taking a measure of your level of fear and letting it be there, not even asking that it go away, actually even embracing it. Remember that the anxiety of stagefright comes from your own struggle reactions. By letting them be there, by not fighting against them, you are stopping the struggle and the feelings will subside.

Another way of learning how to float is to not add frightening thoughts. Instead of saying to yourself "I'm pretty bad now, I don't know what I'll do if this gets worse," floating means accepting your level and saying to yourself, "I'm just going to do what I can with my level of anxiety in the present."

CHAPTER 4: DISTRACTION TECHNIQUES FOR OVERCOMING STAGEFRIGHT

PAUSING

When we fear something, our natural reaction is to speed up, to get through the experience as rapidly as possible. We tend to take a deep breath, grit our teeth, clench our fists and charge through the frightening experience by the sheer force of will. This is called "white knuckling." Yet this very response produces still more anxiety. As we've seen, the behavioral maxim that governs this is "I run, therefore I fear."

An anxious speaker will often begin his talk even before arriving at the lectern. He is off and running, trying to outrun that fear. Of course, since the fear is part of you, you cannot outrun it. What you will end up doing is getting yourself breathless and more anxious before you have finished your first few sentences.

Instead of starting in this manner, you should pause and take command of the lectern and the audience's attention. Do not begin speaking until your level of anxiety is steady or falling, never rising. It is important, of course, that during this period you do not wait impatiently, demanding that your anxiety level go down, as this will only increase it.

During the pause, allow the feelings of anxiety be there. Do not try to push them away, or use the technique of Contact With The Physical Environment to get back into the present.

PARADOXICAL INTENTION

Once you understand the mechanism of stagefright and its origin in thinking that you might get panicky and embarrass yourself, panic can cease to be your enemy and, in fact, can be turned to your advantage. You can actually use your new knowledge of the physiology of stagefright as a means to defeat it.

As with most other physiological phenomena, panic has its purpose in nature. When we become alarmed, our fight or flight responses are activated. When we have received all the disturbing stimuli we can possibly handle, we experience the utmost level of anxiety — a panic. At that point we are totally inwardly focused on ourselves, not even aware of where we are; no additional scary stimuli are received and our anxiety levels brake sharply.

Panic, then, is really the body's self-governing mechanism. Think of it like a safety valve for dealing with excessive fear, somewhat like the safety valve on a residential hot water heater. This little device will rise up to let the steam escape before the whole unit can explode. Similarly, when you panic, you are not aware of anything except your own panic, no stimuli are reaching you. At that point, your body is experiencing its maximum reaction to its catecholamines so your

CHAPTER 4: DISTRACTION TECHNIQUES FOR OVERCOMING STAGEFRIGHT

physiological responses get fatigued and cannot respond further. In this way, panic is self-limiting. It will not kill you, is unlikely to give you a heart attack and cannot make you explode. There are no people confined in mental hospitals because some years ago they experienced a panic attack. People who go to emergency rooms because of a panic attack are typically thrown out because by the time the panic has subsided there is nothing demonstrably wrong with them.

This kind of experience with panic can occur in less time than it would take for a thoughtful or dramatic pause in a presentation, and can even go unnoticed. It is true that some people feel like they have prolonged panic attacks. What has likely happened, however, is that they have experienced the usual quick burst of panic but as soon as it subsided and they got some cognitive function back, they became fascinated by their own panic and wondered, "What was that? Am I going crazy?" Once you understand the dynamics of panic, this is less likely to happen to you. In fact, by understanding the physiological purpose of panic, you can turn this phenomenon to your advantage.

If you find your fear levels are quite high, you can actually try to make them go up, knowing that if you can hit a number 10 on the anxiety scale you will experience panic, at which point your levels will brake sharply and you then can deal with these lower levels using your other distraction techniques. The panic itself will occur in just a few seconds, no longer than it takes for a thought or a pause, and by using your other techniques to prevent your levels from again cycling upward, no one will know what you were experiencing, even in the middle of a speech.

We are making use here of panic as the self-governing safety valve. The apparent paradox is that by trying to make your levels go up, you will actually bring them down!

CHAPTER 5
GOING BLANK AND OTHER SPECIAL CONCERNS

As we saw in Chapter 1 when we considered the causes and physiology of stagefright, the release of catecholamines has profound effects throughout the body, all in support of our fight or flight mechanism. One such effect is the rapid and forceful heartbeat that sends more blood to the skeletal muscles. Another is that the mucous membranes that line the nose and mouth dry out and contract to allow for passage of a greater volume of air. Some people may find one effect more troublesome than others. Others may not have a particular "favorite" symptom and may find all the consequences of stagefright equally troublesome. A few of the particular manifestations of stagefright that tend to be of special concern are discussed below.

GOING BLANK

One of the most common complaints of anxious public speakers is that they go blank or that they are afraid they will go blank and will not be able to recall the information they need. This fear can make impromptu speaking particularly difficult for some people. It also can diminish the effectiveness of a presentation by making you feel that you must read your information so you don't forget it, even though it would actually be more effective and engaging to speak from notes or even without notes.

People with healthy nervous systems do not go blank in the sense of losing information. You do not, all of a sudden in the middle of a public speaking situation, lose information you possess and need. The information is not lost at all, it is there, but there are two thought processes that may prevent you from accessing it.

The first of these processes occurs when, instead of actually losing the information, the person who is afraid of going blank is not able to search for it. Instead, his mind is so filled with the thought, "I am going to go blank," or "I am blank," or "I can't remember," that he is not able to use his intellectual capacity to locate the desired information.

Think of it as if your mind is a computer: The core capacity is so occupied with the thought of going blank that it is not, in fact, carrying out the instructions to locate the needed information. There may not even be any instructions to locate the needed information, only the thoughts related to going blank. In other words, you've stopped doing what you are supposed to be doing.

CHAPTER 5: GOING BLANK AND OTHER SPECIAL CONCERNS

When this happens, it is necessary to push out the thought of being blank so that your mind can locate the needed information. This can be accomplished by using the technique of Staying in the Present by Contact with the Physical Environment, as discussed in the previous chapter.

The second thing that can happen when you think you go blank is that you are trying to see more information at one time than the mind is capable of focusing on. To go back to the analogy of an electronic data processing system, you are trying to display more information on one screen than the screen is capable of showing. The data is there but is must be displayed serially. When you try to focus on the whole, you cannot see specific parts in clarity or detail.

While I remain firm in my own view that the sensation of going blank stems from being distracted by your inner fear-thoughts and not directing your attention to the information you are trying to present, a somewhat different view has recently been proposed.

Neuroscientist Erno Hermans and his collaborators proposed in an article in the November 25, 2011 issue of Science that a mechanism exists by which, as part of the fight or flight response, brain resources may actually be directed away from the higher functioning cerebral cortex areas involved in thought, creativity and planning to other portions of the brain more directed to serving the fight or flight response. Interestingly enough, Hermans credits noradrenaline, a neurotransmitter member of the catecholamine group with mediating this reaction. Thus, it may be whether one subscribes to my philosophy of not paying attention to what you are doing or to Hermans' hypothesis of redirection of brain resources, you are saying much the same thing in only slightly different terms.

The good news is that regardless of which theory of going blank you subscribe to, the solution remains the same. Faced with this sensation, your focus must be brought back to the first syllable of the first word. Since the information is there, once you start, the next bit will be there when it is needed. By getting your attention away from yourself and back to your presentation you are both paying attention to what you are supposed to be doing and also reducing your self-consciousness-induced stress, which should result in a reallocation of brain resources back to the higher cortical functions you need to go forward.

SHAKING HANDS AND LEGS

One of the most disturbing — and to many people embarrassing — reactions that can happen to presenters in front an audience is to have their hands or legs shake. Knocking knees are a dead giveaway of what is going on inside. Even if you are standing behind a lectern so your legs can't be seen, the notion that, all of a sudden, your legs have turned to jelly and can no longer hold you up can be a major cause of discomfort.

CHAPTER 5: GOING BLANK AND OTHER SPECIAL CONCERNS

Of course, nothing of the sort actually happens. Weak, shaky legs are the result of the strain and buckling caused by opposing muscle groups contracting against each other. This is also true of shaky hands, which can be of real concern to someone who has to hold notes, to present or receive an award or to distribute materials to the audience.

In either case, the almost universal response is to tighten up, to put more tension on those muscles. This, of course, only results in making the situation worse. Just as the legs of a normal, healthy person are perfectly capable of holding her steady, a healthy person is capable of holding a few ounces of paper or some other object steady. That is, you are capable of holding steady if you don't start isometrically contracting your muscles against each other in an attempt to steady yourself. If you do this, your arms and legs will buckle and shake.

With practice and using the knowledge you have gained about what causes you to shake, you can avoid the temptation to further contract your muscles against each other when you feel that first tremor. Instead, you can learn to respond by relaxing the tension in the affected arms or legs: When you feel that first unsteadiness, instead of trying to damp it down, you need to let it go. With appropriate prompting, you will be able to remind yourself that your legs are capable of holding you steady without the extra effort you are applying and that you can hold a few ounces in your hands without the extra tightening that results in trembling.

QUIVERING VOICE

Some people are particularly concerned that their voices will quiver or crack. Many fine speakers and media personalities have voices that crack in certain ranges simply as a result of their own vocal architecture. In others, however, it is a reflection of anxiety. Through the same mechanism that affects shaky hands and legs, muscular tissue in the throat also may contract under stress. This can result in a quivering or cracking voice. You may even find yourself talking in a higher pitch when you get excited.

Generally, a cracking or quivering voice caused by contraction of muscles in the throat is responsive to the techniques we have discussed already for relieving overall anxiety in the public speaking environment. When you become more comfortable overall, your throat muscles relax, thus alleviating the problem.

Nevertheless, some people want to specifically address this problem. The first thing to remember is the cause. Since a shaky voice is caused by tension in the muscles in your throat, you want to remind yourself to relax the throat area. Perhaps surprisingly, this relaxation can often be achieved simply by engaging in the conscious realization that you are tightening.

Like people with shaky hands or legs, people with quivering or cracking voices tend to try and control this by tightening up even further. Needless to say, you want to avoid this tendency. One exercise that is helpful, although not suitable for an actual performance situation, is consciously making your voice quiver and crack by raising and lowering your pitch as you practice your presentation. By seeing what it feels like when your voice cracks, you can acquire some control over doing the opposite. At the same time, you can lessen your sensitivity to hearing your voice shake, which in turn will lessen your anxiety and so reduce the likelihood for your voice to be affected when you are actually in the public speaking situation.

DRY MOUTH

Reduced secretions in the mouth and nasopharynx are part of the sympathetic nervous system's response to stress, which results in a dry mouth and throat. Here, again, those general techniques designed to relieve anxiety while giving a presentation will reduce this, although a certain amount of dryness is inevitable from the passage of air when we speak for prolonged periods. Sucking hard candy might seem like an obvious expedient but it is distracting and therefore not appropriate before an audience.

Some people find this dryness intolerable and complain about a clicking sound that may be produced when the mouth is dry. This can be dealt with by a prompting device in the form of a word or phrase to remind you of some favorite food. When the dryness becomes particularly uncomfortable, you can look at your prompting word or phrase. The phrases "strawberry shortcake" or "sour pickle" might be particularly appropriate.

FAINTING

Some stagefright-sufferers are concerned that they will faint during their presentations. Others might actually find such a prospect appealing in that it would release them from being trapped in the public speaking situation, with at least some objective indication that their incapacity was beyond their control.

Fainting, also known as syncope, is extremely unlikely in the course of delivering a presentation. Syncope results from insufficient blood flow reaching the brain as a result of low blood pressure. As we have discussed throughout, stagefright is a consequence of an over-activated sympathetic nervous system response. Most likely the stagefright-sufferer is experiencing increased heart rate resulting in elevated blood pressure, a virtual guarantee against fainting.

To be sure, stagefright is a phobia and some phobic people do pass out. However, that is not the norm. These are people with a fear of needles and injections and possibly of blood. In many cases this reaction is inherited and involves a mechanism that stimulates the vagus nerve, which results in a slowing of the heart and reduced blood pressure (which results in less blood reaching the brain). This is very much the opposite process of what is experienced by most people with stagefright.

In the highly unlikely event that you do pass out during a speech, rest assured that it won't be held against you. Some years back, the famous Watergate judge Leon Jaworski collapsed while giving a speech to a group of lawyers (due to a heart attack, not to stagefright). He was resuscitated by the U.S. Marshal who was escorting him. Somewhat more recently, Commerce Secretary and Presidential Chief of Staff Bill Daley collapsed during a ceremony at the White House. Both men were invited to give presentations on future occasions despite having previously passed out in public.

CHAPTER 6
SOME COGNITIVE ADJUSTMENTS

The essential tools for managing stagefright during a presentation (as opposed to in advance) are your distraction techniques. Only these techniques can provide a satisfactory answer to the two most troubling questions incessantly asked by the stagefright-sufferer: "How do I know that I won't get noticeably nervous as I have before" and, "What if I do get noticeably nervous while I'm giving my presentation?" Only these techniques can derail the stagefright process by distracting you so that you stop the thoughts that inevitably result in catecholamine release.

While your distraction techniques are the primary weapon against stagefright, there are some belief changes that are important over the long run that will help this information "take" better and enable you to apply it more effectively and efficiently. They are cognitive adjustments, changes in the familiar ways that stagefright-sufferers tend to view and think about certain things.

EGO REDUCTION

We have considered how feelings of anxiety arise from the thought that you might embarrass yourself before an audience. People with stagefright typically think of themselves as victims trapped against their wills and having to give a presentation. If, instead, at the time of the presentation we did not attach so much importance to either the presentation or ourselves, our bodies would not react so profoundly to the idea of embarrassment.

In other words, at the same time that we are thinking of ourselves as trapped and helpless victims, there is a part of us that is saying we are really pretty special, that we are capable of perfection, which includes a complete absence of nervousness and that what we do is so important that there is no room for imperfection.

When we blow up our own importance as well as the importance of our presentations, we are increasing our bodies' fight or flight responses in the public speaking arena. As a counter to these feelings of self-importance and perfectionism, it is helpful to get in touch with what it would feel like to give yourself permission to be somewhat less important, perhaps even a little foolish.

Sometimes when working with stagefright groups, I will have someone give a serious speech while holding a rubber chicken or with one of the novelty item headpieces that make it look like you have an arrow through your head. Can you give a serious talk at work while holding a rubber chicken or with an arrow

CHAPTER 6: SOME COGNITIVE ADJUSTMENTS

through your head? In most cases, probably not. What you can do, however, is learn to let yourself feel a bit foolish and not to be so overprotective of your sense of self that you are tripping off your body's emergency responses. In other words, don't put so much importance on yourself.

Just like when you bite the inside of your cheek it swells and tends to get in the way of your teeth, if you go into a presentation situation with an exaggerated idea of your own importance, the importance of what you have to say and the notion that you can achieve perfection in saying it, you are increasing and sustaining your public speaking anxiety levels.

ACCEPTANCE

Now for some more good news — and bad news. First, the bad news. Stagefright tends to be a continuing problem. As we have discussed, it is helpful for people with stagefright to think of themselves in somewhat the same way that people with an alcohol problem must think of themselves: You can lead a normal life and function appropriately when you do the things you are supposed to do and when you stay away from the things you must avoid. However, most people are never really totally cured. This is because at any given time you can resort to your old, self-conscious thoughts and awareness, giving yourself an immediate catecholamine infusion, with the consequent physical results. Just as an alcoholic probably shouldn't ever take another drink, the person with stagefright must stay away from fear-thinking and not indulge that thought of "What if I embarrass myself?"

Now it's time for the good news. The more you accept that you have stagefright and that sometimes you may get panicky when speaking before an audience, the less panicky you will get. You may think, "But I don't want to accept it, it's not acceptable to me to get panicky." You must remember that stagefright has to do with your own fight or flight or struggle reactions. The more you struggle against the panicky feelings, the stronger they become. Conversely, the more you accept them, the less you are struggling and the lower your anxiety level is going to be. Bottom line: Acceptance pays off.

IT'S NOT ALWAYS ABOUT YOU

Any good teacher learns from his students. This particular insight came from a student who shared it with our group. Most presentations are not about you (there are exceptions, of course; you might, for example, have to give a defense of a thesis for an academic degree). You are merely a means to deliver some information that someone has determined a group needs to have. You may be presenting the speech because it's part of your job, because you're the one who knows specific information or because you're the person who is available at the time. The central understanding is that it is the *information* that is important and is the real star of the show. You are just an instrument, a kind of audio-visual aid like a microphone or projector to get it across. This stands in contrast to the mindset of someone with stagefright, as discussed when we considered the NASCAR Assumption, that the reason you have been assigned to give a presentation is because people enjoy seeing gruesome train wrecks.

MARGIN OF SAFETY

One of the hardest things to convince a stagefright-sufferer is that he has any margin of safety at all. People with stagefright tend to believe that their physical reactions are entirely transparent to the audience and it is very difficult to persuade them otherwise. This is really not surprising when you are trying to contradict what that person knows he is experiencing in his own body.

To be sure, someone with stagefright can, at some point, become noticeably uncomfortable but it's not likely to be happening when you first feel it. You are the only one stuffed inside your particular skin so naturally you can feel the early, first effects of your catecholamine intoxication but that doesn't mean the effects are, at that point, perceptible to others.

You may feel some muscle fibers tightening up, but considerable bundles of fibers must contract against the bundles in the opposing muscles before you develop noticeable trembling that anyone else might observe. This means that pretty much every time you have given a presentation, you have had a misleading experience in that you have what you believe is accurate information coming from your body but you have no reliable information coming from outside sources. If you seek feedback from audience members you are very unlikely to accept any positive reports as anything but polite lies. For instance, if someone with stagefright asked a friend or colleague, "Did I seem nervous?" and the friend replied, "No, you were fine," the likely reaction would be for the stagefright-sufferer to think, "He is just trying to be nice but he's a terrible liar."

We have found that the only way to overcome this information bias is to videotape people, when they are sufficiently ready, so they can get a more objective experience of how other people perceive them. One of the surprising things I have found from this is that there is not a particularly good correlation between any overt nervousness people display and their sense of stagefright discomfort. A significant number of people with stagefright display very little, if any, physical reactions. It may well be people's own internal perceptions that are causing them to suffer.

The margin of safety available to stagefright-sufferers is illustrated by an experiment that is an established part of stagefright lore: An auditorium was reportedly filled with subjects who were given questionnaires to rate their perception of a speaker's level of anxiety. The results are said to have found a

CHAPTER 6: SOME COGNITIVE ADJUSTMENTS

direct correlation between the distance between the speaker and the audience member. Those up front concluded that perhaps the speaker was just a little nervous, those in the middle saw virtually no anxiety and those at the back experienced the speaker as totally poised.

FORGIVING YOURSELF

In Chapter 3 I discussed the importance of forgiving yourself and not obsessing over and mentally punishing yourself for a bad experience. This is one cognitive adjustment that everyone with stagefright must make.

Perhaps the most malignant aspect of stagefright is the way in which each perceived failure predisposes you to the next. If you "indulge" in recriminations such as, "Everyone could see I was nervous, and somebody even told me so," "They think there's something wrong with me," "I should have, I would have, I could have," you are not just *not* helping yourself, you are aggravating any damage that might actually have been done.

If there were any benefit to be achieved from this form of self-punishment, no one would have stagefright; everyone would be cured, because we all tend to engage in that kind of thinking. All you are doing is mentally putting more chips on the table, raising the stakes for next time. When you return to the question of, "How do I know I won't have a bad experience as I did before," you have this to add to it, "Remember how much you suffered after the last bad experience? This could be even worse." You have now conditioned yourself to heighten your fear responses, putting yourself at greater risk.

Life is not like a videotape that you can rewind. Once an event has taken place, it cannot be undone. If you have a bad experience, the only option available is to immediately forgive yourself and move on. The only thing that can be achieved by not doing so is to dig a deeper hole. As the saying goes, when you find yourself in a hole, the first thing to do is to stop digging. The more you can assure yourself that you will forgive yourself if you have a bad experience, the more your problem will diminish. The positive step you take to avoid a repetition of the bad outcome is to apply the information you are receiving here.

CHAPTER 7
THE STAGEFRIGHT MEDICINE CHEST

As we know, stagefright is essentially a chemical problem. As so aptly described by investigators Charles Otto Brantigan and T.A. Brantigan, it is a self-poisoning with one's own catecholamines, the chemical substances that initiate and govern the fight or flight response. Ultimately, whether we are using cognitive-behavioral means or other chemical substances, we are accomplishing the same thing: manipulating the body's production and release of catecholamines.

Catecholamines are biologically active organic molecules. That is, they are compounds built primarily of carbon with similar chemical structures and pathways of synthesis and metabolism. They serve both as hormones, substances that are delivered into the bloodstream by endocrine glands, and as neurotransmitters, which are substances that pass from nerve cell to nerve cell across the synapses (spaces between these cells). The neurotransmitters transmit messages along the nervous system by this method.

Perhaps the most familiar of these catecholamines is epinephrine, also called adrenaline, familiar to anyone who has ever watched a television emergency room drama. In these shows, a patient whose heart is stopping is wheeled in on a gurney and someone yells, "Quick, get me an ampoule of 'epi.'" If epinephrine is such a powerful stimulant that it can reactivate an arrested heart, you can imagine what a powerful effect it and its chemical cousins have on a person who is not in cardiac arrest but is merely trying to give a talk.

Another member of the catecholamines is norepinephrine, or noradrenaline, which can also be released as a hormone into the blood. It also is a chemical messenger within the nervous system and sends messages from one neuron to another. Much like a conditioned reflex, catecholamines are produced when you think you are in danger, even if the danger is only the social danger of embarrassing yourself. The process is similar to how your body produces saliva unconsciously when you think about food, regardless of whether there is any food around, Even just a moment of self-concious awareness can have this reflexive effect.

As we have previously discussed, catecholamines are powerful stimulants. One of their effects can be a spacey, disconnected feeling called "depersonalization reaction" in which you feel like you are looking down on yourself from a position floating around the ceiling of the room. It is possible that this spacey, depersonalization reaction is related to the effect that catecholamines have in increasing the levels of glucose in the blood to provide energy in preparation for the anticipated fight or flight.

CHAPTER 7: THE STAGEFRIGHT MEDICINE CHEST

Before we discuss substances that can affect stagefright for better or worse, we should note one substance that isn't supposed to affect it, or indeed, anything at all, but does — placebo.

PLACEBO

A placebo is an inert substance that has no known physiological effect. On some ocasions, placebos have been used with the objective of achieving a beneficial result, such as relieving pain. Most importantly, plecebos are used as controls in scientific experiments that aim to determine whether a specific substance has any medicinal value. In other words, for a substance to be regarded as effective and therefore of further interest, it must prove itself statistically better than nothing — that is, better than the plecebo. If the results achieved with the active, candidate substance are not significantly better than the plecebo, it is regarded as having no pharmacological value.

The gold standard in judging the effectiveness of a candidate drug is called a double blind, crossover study. In this kind of experiment, neither the experimenter nor the subject knows who is getting the substance being tested and who is getting the placebo; that information is kept coded until the experiment is concluded. If subjects respond to the candidate substance with statistically significant superior results, the candidate substance may then be administered to the subjects who previously received the plecebo. This will help confirm the efficacy of the tested substance.

A problem arises, however, because up to 30 percent of the general population is susceptible to the "placebo effect," which means that they will report a beneficial experience simply as a result of them thinking they may be receiving a medication. The placebo effect may also be boosted because the subject is responding to getting attention from the experimenter.

Further confounding the placebo effect is what has been termed the "nocebo effect," which is the experiencing of negative reactions by subjects who are being given placebos. It is not uncommon in drug trials for a certain percentage of subjects receiving the dummy drug to complain to the experimentors, "I can't take this stuff anymore, Doc, its too strong" or "It's making me worse," or "It's making me sick" and even to drop out of the study.

An understanding of the placebo effect is important in the context of stagefright because it is necessary to understand the discussion of substances that follows and to evaluate other suggested approaches to stagefright as discussed more fully in Chapter 12.

The placebo effect also has a specific and direct tie to stagefright. As we have seen, stagefright is intiated by thoughts or awareness of the social danger of being embarrassed or humiliating one's self. Anything that made such thoughts unsustainable would have a positive impact on stagefright. If you were convinced that under no circumstances could you embarrass yourself, you would not release the catecholamines that are responsible for the physical reactions of stagefright.

For example, if a person with stagefright were to convince himself that swinging a dead cat around his head three times would cure his stagefright, he very likely would get a positive result if he tried this method. A stagefright-sufferer who performed the "dead cat" procedure would no longer be susceptible to the thought that he could embarrass himself by appearing nervous and would therefore not release the catecholamines that, in fact, initiate the physical reactions of nervousness.

It is very important to keep the placebo effect and its particular application to stagefright in mind when evaluating not only the chemicals that may be available to address the problem, but also other management approaches that may be offered. If you really believed that you were stagefright "bulletproof," you would not get it. On the other hand, would you really want to risk your success in giving presentaions on something that was held up only by your belief in it?

ALCOHOL

People have probably been self-medicating themselves with alcohol for stagefright for as long as there have been people, alcohol and stagefright. Alcohol is a drug with significant central nervous system depressant effects. It dulls your thinking, including the kind of fear-thinking that initiates stagefright, as well as feeling and motor skills. Given its widespread availability, it is, therefore, not surprising that stagefright-sufferers have too often resorted to alcohol for relief.

Alcohol is a particularly bad drug for stagefright because its side effects and dosing are unmanageable. Too little and it may not have an adequate effect. Too much and you are unable to give your presentation at all. Worse still is if you drink too much alcohol and then engage in inappropriate behavior that is in itself embarrassing (even though you may not realize it until sometime later). Alcohol also doesn't maintain a steady level of relief for long enough to be of much use for stagefright. And why would you want to take something to ease anxiety in giving a presentation when a significant side effect of that substance is not being able to give your presentation very well or even at all?

CHAPTER 7: THE STAGEFRIGHT MEDICINE CHEST

Sadly, at one time it was not uncommon to see someone with stagefright who had also worked herself into an alcohol problem as well. Moreover, it is highly likely that someone known to be consuming alcohol before giving a presentation would not be regarded sympathetically as someone coping with stagefright but instead would be viewed critically, as a person with poor impulse control.

Alcohol is also capable of some other side effects that make it particularly inappropriate as a stagefright treatment. Possibly because of its dehydrating effects and possibly because of a rebound effect as the alcohol wears off, some people find themselves even more jittery after having had a drink than they would have been if they had not consumed alcohol at all. This can be particularly unfortunate since it is not always possible to adhere to the schedule of when you are expected to speak.

The difficulties with using alcohol as a drug for stagefright management can perhaps best be illustrated by the old joke about the young priest who was going to deliver his first sermon but was greatly troubled by stagefright. It is of concededly dubious taste, but possibly best makes the point.

The young priest was consumed by anticipatory anxiety and shared his concern with a more experienced colleague. The more experienced priest advised the younger man to keep a glass of vodka at the alter to ease his nervousness. The young priest did so, completing the service with the feeling that he had done a creditable job. Later, he received a critique from his older colleague that made the following points:

> Father,
> (1) In the future, sip, don't gulp; (2) we do not refer to the cross as the "big T thing"; and (3) we do not refer to Our Lord as "the Big Daddy." Finally, next Saturday, the Girl Scout Troop will be holding a taffy-pulling contest at St. Peter's, not a peter-pulling contest at St. Taffy's.

In these days of high dietary consciousness I am frequently asked about diet in connection with stagefright. The one piece of advice I would consistently offer is don't drink alcohol if you are going to be called upon to give a presentation. Certainly, in the twenty-first century no one should be medicating herself with alcohol in order to give a talk.

BENADRYL

One substance that is occasionally mentioned but that is probably as poor a choice as alcohol is Benadryl. Benadryl is a very powerful, early generation antihistaminic drug used to treat allergic conditions. It is extremely sedating so it does have powerful depressive effects on your central nervous system that might make it appear to mask anxiety symptoms. Unfortunately it is also a hypnotic, which means it can cause spacey, dissociative, almost hallucinogenic-like effects. Because of its hypnotic and highly soporific properties, Benadryl is inappropriate for performance situations. In addition, it is capable of paradoxical effects, meaning it can cause the opposite reaction in some people, such as agitation, especially in very young people.

CAFFEINE

Caffeine is unquestionably a psychoactive, stimulant drug that acts on the central nervous system. It increases the levels of the powerful stimulant epinephrine/adrenaline and can itself mimic the effects of epinephrine. One of its "metabolites," meaning one of the components that caffeine breaks down into, is theophylline, which has a very powerful stimulant effect on the heart. At very large dossages, more than even an avid coffee drinker is normally likely to imbibe, the stimulant effects of caffeine are toxic and can even be lethal.

That said, people's senstivity to caffeine varies widely. We all have friends or acquantances who will decline a cup of coffee late in the day because of their experience that it will interfere with their ability to go to sleep that night. Many other people are not so affected.

The best that can be said for the role of caffeine in stagefright is that it is likely to follow a person's experience with it outside the presentation environment. People who are sensitive to caffeine in general may find that it aggrevates their anxiety in giving a presentation. Others may find that it doesn't make much difference one way or the other. Abstaining from coffee, tea, colas and other caffeinated beverages on the day of a presentation is probably an experiment worth trying. An exception would be in the case of those who have regularly consumed large amounts of caffeine. Because you develop a tolerance to caffeine, an abrupt halt to consuming it could trigger a withdrawal reaction that would not be desirable in conjunction with giving a presentation.

BETA BLOCKERS

Without any doubt the single biggest contribution to the understanding and management of stagefright was made by the Brantigan brothers, the brilliant and accomplished, polymath, surgeon, researcher, musician, historical preservationist and civic leader Dr. Charles Otto Brantigan, M.D., and his brother, T.A. Brantigan, whose doctorate is in musical arts. Their work with stagefright set a milestone. It provides the scientific basis for the use of beta blockers in managing stagefright and, even more important, it provides scientific proof of the role of catecholamines in stagefright, confirming the phenomena as, in their words, "a self-poisoning with one's own catecholamines."

CHAPTER 7: THE STAGEFRIGHT MEDICINE CHEST

The compound propranolol was first synthesized by a Scotsman, Sir James Whyte Black, in the late 1950s. (Dr. Black was also the first to synthesize the stomach acid blocking compound cimetidine, known under the brand name of Tagamet. His work was recognized some 30 years later with the Nobel Prize for Medicine.) Propranolol belongs to a class of compounds called beta blockers because of their effect on beta adrenergic receptor sites. Receptor sites can be thought of in functional terms as keyholes in the membranes that surround cells. Chemical keys that fit these receptor keyholes can unlock the cell membrane and induce chemical reactions that affect the cell or cause it to do various things.

As we have seen, catecholamines are chemical keys that can fit into receptor site keyholes and trigger the increased heart rate, changes in breathing rhythm and trembling that are the hallmarks of stagefright. Beta blockers like propranolol fit into the same keyholes (the beta adrenergic receptor sites) as catecholamines. Unlike catecholamines, however, the beta blocker keys can only fit into the keyhole, they cannot turn the lock. That means that when a catecholamine key comes along and encounters a beta adrenergic receptor keyhole that is already occupied by a beta blocker key, it cannot gain entrance and cause the physiological reactions of stagefright. The catecholamine key is then broken down by the body into other substances and removed. Some people describe their experience of having a fear-thought while taking propranolol like turning the key in a car with a dead battery: you hear a click but the engine doesn't turn over.

Although other uses for propranolol have subsequently been found (it treats migraines, for example), it was first approved and marketed for hypertension to lower high blood pressure. Physicians later discovered so-called "off label" uses, meaning they found that beta blockers were useful for other conditions for which they were not originally intended, tested or approved. Once a pharmaceutical has been released on the market, there are no legal restrictions on using it for other purposes. This allows medicines that have been determined to be tolerably safe for one indication to be experimented with for other possible uses without the prohibitive expense of testing that is incurred with respect to a new drug.

After propranolol reached the market, people noticed that in addition to its beneficial effect on high blood pressure, it also reduced tremors. In fact, it is still used to treat certain tremors, particularly in the elderly. According to urban legend, the first physicians to seize upon this anti-tremor effect were ophthalmologic surgeons who need very steady hands in the delicate procedures they performed. Physicians can also suffer from stagefright and soon it became known within the medical profession that propranolol was helpful not only in performing delicate surgery but also in the equally challenging task of giving a presentation to a medical society. While this use of propranolol was whispered among doctors, up until then no scientific experimentation had been conducted to establish the efficacy of propranolol for this purpose.

CHAPTER 7: THE STAGEFRIGHT MEDICINE CHEST

In 1980, the Brantigan brothers, together with their collaborator, Dr. N. Joseph, carried out a double-blind crossover study of the effects of 40 mg of propranolol taken one and a half hours before a musical recital. Thirteen subjects were tested at the University of Nebraska Music Department and an additional 16 were subsequently tested at the Julliard School of Music in New York.[2]

The subjects were monitored for outward signs of stagefright during their performances and their own reactions were recorded using questionnaires. The study concluded that beta blockers effectively reduced the physical manifestations of stagefright and thereby actually led to an improved musical performance.

In another arm of the Brantigans' study, participants were offered the opportunity to experience the beta stimulator called terbutaline. Wisely, only seven study subjects wished to do so. The stimulator increased stagefright and, as one study subject put it, "the less said about this pill the better."

The Brantigans' contribution to the understanding of stagefright consists not only in identifying propranolol as useful in managing stagefright but in confirming the stagefright mechanism of catecholamines. Dr. Charles Otto Brantigan's seminal work on stagefright and beta blockade has been published and presented to multiple prestigious professional groups in the musical and medical fields.[3]

Although some beta blocker molecules are small enough to pass through the blood-brain barrier, the membranes that prevent certain chemicals from passing from the bloodstream to the brain itself, we like to think of propranol as acting from the neck down. That is, it doesn't have tranquilizing effects when used to

---

[2] The Nebraska subjects consisted largely of music students from nearby colleges and universities. The audience consisted of other participants and faculty members. On the second day of the Nebraska study, a television crew was brought in to tape the performances. At Juilliard, the subjects consisted of members of the New York Philharmonic Orchestra, Juilliard students and professional musicians who were interested in the stagefright problem. The audience consisted of a few interested members of the orchestra and Juilliard staffs.

[3] The Brantigans presented their research to: Stage Fright and the Professional Musician, University of Colorado Department of Surgery Centennial Celebration, Starzl Day, May 25, 1983; Beta Blocking Drugs in the Treatment of Stage Fright, Conference on Medical Problems of Musicians, Aspen Music Festival, Aspen, Colorado, July 28-August 1, 1983; Stage Fright: Characteristics, Physiology and the Role of Beta Sympathetic Receptors in Its Modification, Second International Conference on Tension in Performance, Kingston Upon Thames, United Kingdom, July 24-27, 1983; Beta Blocking Drugs in the Treatment of Stage Fright, Symposium on the Treatment of Anxiety and Panic, Royal Free Hospital Academic Department of Medicine, London, England, July 23, 1983; Brantigan, TA, Brantigan, CO. Stage fright characteristics, physiology and the role of beta sympathetic receptors in its modification. Journal ISSTP 1:13-20 (1984); and Brantigan, TA, Brantigan, CO, Beta blockade and stage fright, looking back. Int. Trumpet Guild J 8:20-22. 1984.

CHAPTER 7: THE STAGEFRIGHT MEDICINE CHEST

help manage stagefright. Although chronic regular beta blocker administration, such as is used for high blood pressure patients, can have a side effect of tiredness, acute administration such as is done for occasional use does not produce the same sleepiness. Nor does using beta blockers diminish intellectual sharpness like tranquilizers can.

Another distinction between tranquilizers and beta blockers as described in the Brantigan study is that the beta blocker reduced the subjects' "situational anxiety" or (their "states") but not their overall level of anxiety or (their "traits."). Dr. David L. Charney, the co-founder of the Stagefright Survival School, describes the following situational effect of using beta blockers this way: Because the stagefright-sufferer fears that others will preceive the outward signs of his nervousness, when those signs are reduced by beta blockade, there is an overall reduction in anxiety. As Dr. Charney describes it, "The brain checks in with the body. The body says 'There's nothing much going on down here,' so the brain concludes that there isn't that much to worry about." Dr. Charney calls this "the backdoor tranquilizer effect."

The 40 mg used in the Brantigan study probably represents the upper range of the useful dose of propranol for stagefright, even though much larger dosages are used to treat people with high blood pressure. Taking the medication one and a half hours before a presentation, as done in the Brantigan study, seems to be the safe margin for using the beta blocker prior to a presentation. The effect seems to last for about 4 hours after it is absorbed, meaning that it remains effective for about five and a half hours after you take it.

As is the case with all medications, the dosages of propranolol can be widely variable and require individual adjustment. Some people appear to be sensitve to propranolol at what would appear to be sub-clinical doses, while others require higher doses. Dosing for stagefright is confounded by the dynamic nature of the process: Because stagefright, the fear of embarrassing yourself by appearing inappropriately nervous, feeds upon itself, it is always a moving target. There is a constant adjustment between the anti-stagefright chemicals a person has taken and the catecholamines that he or she produces during a public-speaking situation.

The level of propranolol that may feel just adequate when you begin a presentation may feel like overmedication later in the speech as you reduce your catecholamine production in response to the realization that you are proceeding successfully and the danger has passed. The effect of overmedication with propranolol can be a sort of stunned, robotic feeling as if you were slowly coming out of a deep freeze.

CHAPTER 7: THE STAGEFRIGHT MEDICINE CHEST

There doesn't seem to be any relationship between size/weight and sensitivity to stagefright medication. Some very large men have claimed to be exquisitely sensitive to propranolol and some petite women have required the upper level of doseage. Even among people who, through the same cognitive pattern, end up with stagefright, some are more "tightly wound" than others.

Despite its undoubted utility, propranolol or any beta blocker is hardly the be all and end all of stagefright. Over the years we have had any number of people at our school who have had access to all the propranolol they could have possibly needed, either as treatment for high blood pressure or otherwise. However, without adding distraction techniques, a number of them have found it ineffective. Based on their experience, their reaction to a discussion of beta blockers is, "Oh, that doesn't work for me." In contrast to taking medication alone, the use of beta blockers together with the application of distraction techniques is highly effective.

As mentioned earlier, the situation seems to be not unlike finding standing water from a leaking pipe in your basement. You can mop and bail it out but if you don't stop the source of the leaks, you end up pretty much chasing your tail. First, you need to find the source of the leak and shut it off or patch it up, then you can mop up and have the use of your basement again.

In stagefright you need to reduce your own production and release of catecholamines by using the techniques to distract yourself from the kind of self-conscious awareness and fear of embarrassment that causes you to produce them. Otherwise you are merely engaging in chemical warfare with yourself.

Just as beta blockers compete against catecholamines, it is reasonable to expect that catecholamines compete against beta blockers. Therefore, if you don't change your thinking and get your mind off of your self, you can continue to pour out catecholamines. Your body is a more efficient chemical manufacturing plant than the ones built by pharmaceutical companies. That means that at some point you can flood the level of blockade protection you have achieved with beta blockers. If you reduce your own catecholamine production by using our cognitive-behavioral techniques to distract yourself, the blocking effect of propranolol has a much better chance to help.

No one wants to take, and no physician wants to prescribe daily medication to cover the off chance that you might find yourself in a presentation situation. At the same time, you never can tell when someone may stop by your desk and say, "A situation has developed and we need you to come to the conference room and tell the people assembled there about the work you have been doing." When that happens, you don't want to have to say, "Okay, let me clear my desk and I'll be there in an hour and a half when my pill kicks in." While medications can and

CHAPTER 7: THE STAGEFRIGHT MEDICINE CHEST

do have a useful role to play, the management of stagefright must begin with an understanding of the process, where it comes from and what causes it, and what you have to do to manage your thinking so that you can control it.

ALPRAZOLAM

Alprazolam is the second of the two medications with particular importance in stagefright. It belongs to the benzodiazepine class of psychoactive drugs. That is, it is a minor tranquilizer. All the drugs of this class slow down the central nervous system and, to one extent or another, have hypnotic, sedative, relaxing, anticonvulsant, muscle relaxant and amnesic properties. Alprazolam is a chemical cousin to the first synthesized members of the group, Librium and Valium. (You can read about my own experience with using Librium to fight stagefright in Chapter 9.)

Chlordiazepoxide, best known as Librium, was first discovered in 1954 by the Austrian scientist Leo Sternbach (1908–2005), who was working on dyes for the Hoffmann–La Roche pharmaceutical company. Little attention was paid to the compound until 1957 when it was found to be an effective tranquilizer. It reached the market some three years later. Diazepam, the second of these "benzos," came along in 1963.

Alprazolam was patented by UpJohn, now Pfizer, Inc., in 1976 and reached the market in 1981 and was intended for use for panic disorders. While there are more than a dozen benzodiazepine prescription drugs available in the United States, Alprazolam is particularly applicable to stagefright because of its pharmacokinetic profile: It goes to work fairly rapidly, perhaps in as little as 45 minutes, and is considered short-acting. Among benzos, short-acting agents are those with a half-life of less than 12 hours, meaning that half of the drug has been metabolized to an inactive state within that time.

In contrast to the beta blockers like propranolol, alprazolam most definitely acts on your head with an anxiolytic effect, meaning it reduces anxiety. While propranolol tends to reduce the quick heart rate, hyperventilation and tremulousness of stagefright, alprazolam can be thought of as reducing the self-conciousness and thoughts of embarrassment that cause the release of catecholamines that initate stagefright's physical manifestations. In other words, alprazolam acts on the mental portion of stagefright and propranolol acts on the physiological results of stagefright.

Taking alprazolam makes it easier to use the distraction techniques because it makes the self-concsious thoughts of embarrassing yourself less compelling. It makes the kind of fear-thoughts that are responsible for stagefright less obsessional. In a sense, taking alprazolam makes these kinds of thoughts less "sticky" so it is easier to stay fully focused on your presentation, which helps shut down stagefright.

Alprazolam does, however, somewhat reduce alertness. Taking too much can be intoxicating so avoiding overdose is particularly important. As we saw with propranolol, because of the dynamic chemical nature of stagefright, what may be an appropriate dose for comfort at the beginning of a presentation may result in sleepiness as your anxiety is reduced from the positive feedback of a successfully proceeding performance. Like all medications, people's sensitivity to this drug also can vary widely regardless of objective factors such as height and weight. Some people may be exquisitely sensitive and others much less so.

Because of alprazolam's sedative side effects, taking it during the day can sometimes be problematic if, after a presentation, you have to work in a quiet environment. You don't want to have to fight to stay awake for the rest of your workday. As was true for propranolol, alprazolam has a place in controlling stagefright but its place is limited.

No one would want to constantly take tranquilizers in case of an occasional presentation and no medical professional would want to put someone constantly in that state. At the same time a presentation experience may sometimes occur on short notice in the workplace. Much like with propranolol, the role of alprazolam is solely as an adjunct to learning to control stagefright through application of cognitive-behavioral techniques to distract yourself from your self-conscious thoughts.

Alprazolam also has another important role it can play. Although the ultimate solution to anticipatory anxiety is confidence based on past success, alprazolam can be useful in managing anxiety and preventing nervous suffering and loss of sleep in advance of a scheduled presentation. If you take alprazolam during the day in the hours before a presentation, careful attention to dosage must be observed to prevent becoming sedated prior to the speech.

My cofounder at the Stagefright Survival School, Dr. David Charney, likes to think of both of these substances as training wheels, or perhaps as a chemical safety net for new and particularly challenging situations. Most of the time it will be appropriate for most people to rely solely on their distraction techniques. Sometimes it will be appropriate for some people to have the addition of one, the other, or both of these medications.

YES, WE HAVE NO BANANAS

Run a Google search on "stagefright and bananas" and see what you come up with. There are pages of hits. Apparently there are many people who seriously believe that eating bananas has a useful role in addressing stagefright. Of course, we know about the placebo effect.

If someone tells you that something you ingest will have a beneficial effect on stagefright he ought to at least be able to tell you how it works. Some of these hits refer to potassium and even mention its role in neurotransmission. But naming something and even saying that it has something to do with something else isn't the same as explaining how it works.

Yes, bananas are a good source of dietary potassium, which is necessary for good health. On the other hand, too much potassium will kill you and can be used to dispatch condemned prisoners by lethal injection. There is no particular reason to believe that people who suffer stagefright are deficient in potassium. How then would potassium from bananas or anywhere else help?

Until someone can adequately explain the benefits of bananas and offer the sort of scientific proof that the Brantigan brothers provided with respect to the effects of beta blockade, I will have to remain skeptical.

I believe that the thinking of the banana crowd is reflective of the kind of thought processes my late father was prone to. Dad was also a big believer in the salutary effects of bananas. Bananas, like other fruits, undoubtedly have a place in a healthy diet, but it is the reason that Dad had concluded that bananas were especially good for you that warrants attention.

Dad had seen a TV documentary on the work of the saintly Dr. Albert Schweitzer who performed missionary work in Africa. Apparently, upon discharge from his hospital, each convalescent patient was given a bunch of bananas. Dad had accordingly concluded that if this famous doctor prescribed bananas for his patients, then they must surely have special health benefits.

As far as I have been able to ascertain, Schweitzer was justly famous as a great humanitarian. He made limitless personal sacrifices to care for an impoverished, medically underserved population under very difficult conditions. He does not, however, seem to be known for any particular contribution to medical science. When his malnourished patients left his hospital, he gave them what he had readily at hand, which, since he was in Africa, happened to be bananas. Schweitzer was Swiss. Had he been working in his home country and followed his practice of using readily available, local resources, Dad no doubt would have become a believer in the special health benefits of chocolate and Swiss cheese.

THAT'S NUTS

According to popular press reports, scientists working in Slovakia administered three grams each of the amino acids lysine and arginine to test subjects and a similar volume of placebo to a control group before each of the groups gave presentations. According to the reports, blood measurements of stress hormones indicated that the test subjects were only half as anxious as the control group during and after their speeches. Arginine can be found in nuts and lysine is in many foods, including yogurt.

Properly conducted research into the biochemistry of stagefright advances our knowledge and is always welcome. I would, however, strongly caution against individual experimentation with amino acid supplements without adequate medical supervision. Overloading on amino acids can have adverse health effects. In addition, contrary to popular belief, dietary supplements are not subject to the same rigorous regulation as pharmaceuticals are. In the late 1980s, for example, the amino acid tryptophan entered the U.S. market with suggestions that it had beneficial properties as a sleep aid and as an anxiety-reducing agent. Within a few months, 37 people died and more than 1,500 were permanently disabled by a toxin created during the tryptophan manufacturing process.

As of this writing, the efficacy of banana-nut bread in the management of stagefright remains unknown.

VALERIAN

Valerian is an herbal preparation made from the root of a flowering perennial plant called *Valeriana officinalis* (at least, that's what it's supposed to be made from). It is one of the herbal preparations most commonly mentioned in connection with stagefright. The herb is said to have anxiety-reducing properties. Anyone considering trying Valerian should bear in mind the placebo effect we have previously discussed, as well as the lack of regulation and standardization that applies to all supplements.

VITAMINS

Practically every nutritional substance from vitamin A to zinc has been suggested at one time or another as exerting a positive influence on controlling stagefright. Vitamins B and C are said to lessen stagefright symptoms when taken on a regular basis. Calcium and magnesium are said to calm the nerves. The truth is that the effect of dietary supplements on stagefright is the same as it is on everything else that the vitamins have been applied to. There is no known benefit to any vitamin or mineral aside from treating or preventing a deficiency of that vitamin or mineral.

OTHER STUFF

There is virtually a limitless number of other chemical compounds that depress the central nervous system or have anxiolytic (anxiety-reducing) effects. There

CHAPTER 7: THE STAGEFRIGHT MEDICINE CHEST

are numerous volumes that address psychotropic drugs, which are substances that affect the mind and therefore potentially affect stagefright. These substances include all of the other benzos, traditional antidepressants called tricyclics and the more recent line of antidepressants called selective serotonin reuptake inhibitors (SSRIs). However, I have specifically included in this book only the substances we have already discussed because of their special and particular relevance in stagefright.

We have discussed placebo because it is important for people with stagefright to understand its effect in evaluating the many other models and treatment modalities that are offered to them. It has special applicability to stagefright because anything that genuinely convinced you that you were not in danger would, in fact, have efficacy. We have talked about caffeine and alcholol because they are ubiquitous and can have a significant effect on the problem. Finally, we have discussed beta blockers, particularly propranolol, and benzodiazepines, particularly alprazolam, because their use is supported by scientific studies and extensive clinical experience.

MEDITATIONS ON MEDICATIONS

During the 2008 Olympic Games in Beijing, the press reported that North Korean shooter Kim Jong Su had tested positive for taking propranolol. This caused him to be disqualified and stripped of his silver and bronze medals. Propranolol is a banned substance at the Olympics; it is tested for and is detectable. Why did Kim Jong Su run this risk? Did he have stagefright? Obviously we don't really know the answer to this question but it allows us to consider some questions.

Beta blockers are banned from the Olympics because they are thought to give the people who use them an unfair advantage, particularly in hand-eye coordination sports such as shooting and archery. The idea is that, by reducing tremors that might lower the accuracy of a shooter's aim and possibly by slowing down his heart rate, a competitor could take his shot at his steadiest and between heartbeats.

Suppose Kim Jong Su didn't take the beta blocker to gain an unfair advantage. Suppose he took it for stagefright because he was so affected that despite his skill he was unable to compete in front of Olympic crowds without this help. Would you say, "If he does poorly because of stagefright he doesn't deserve to win a medal any more than if he had not turned in a winning performance?" The cellist Sara Sant'Ambrogio, who plays in the group Eroica Trio, says, "If you have to take a drug to do your job, then go get another job." I disagree.

What if Kim Jong Su took the beta blocker because he had high blood pressure

CHAPTER 7: THE STAGEFRIGHT MEDICINE CHEST

and was in danger of having a stroke during the competition. Should he be disqualified then? What if he had asthma and needed asthma medication, which is also among the Olympics' banned substances? Should asthmatics be unable to compete just because they have to take medicine?

What about analgesics, the pain relievers that injured athletes are given? Does that give them an advantage over an injured player who plays in pain? What about all the elaborate braces and appliances they wear on the field? Does that give them an advantage over an uninjured player who doesn't have the extra protection these devices may provide?

Where do you draw the line between something that "enhances" performance and something that is necessary to put competitors on an even playing field? The fact is that while all of us are unique human beings capable of many wonderful things, at some level at least, we are each a walking chemical soup. If the ingredients in your particular soup are not up to a particular task, whether it's an Olympic competition or giving a presentation, shouldn't you be able to adjust the recipe, by adding a little salt perhaps, to make the soup more satisfying? The concern that is always expressed, of course, is that you are providing the person who can add to the ingredients in his soup an unfair advantage.

We may never know why Kim Jong Su took propranolol. What we do know is that any opinionated viewpoint about the use of medication in relation to any aspect of performance, including stagefright, is bound to be wrong. Any such decision must take into account the answers to the questions raised above and then can only be made by someone who can say she has walked a mile in a stagefright-sufferer's shoes. While it is highly desirable not to rely on medication in presentation situations, no one should ever feel that he is somehow "cheating" if, on occasion, he finds it necessary to use the medications.

CHAPTER 8
DRILLS, SKILLS AND EXERCISES

Obviously it is simply not possible to completely transform ten weeks of intensive personal coaching, plus as many additional sessions as are needed, for overcoming stagefright into a book. Nevertheless, there are some drills and exercises that students are encouraged to do on their own at home that are helpful.

TIMED READINGS

We ask the student to choose something to read aloud alone at home. It doesn't matter very much what it is; a selection from a book, magazine or newspaper is fine. Read aloud for five minutes. Write the word "slow" or "slow down" on a sticky note you can see while you are reading or in the margins of your text. Then go back and concentrate on slowing down so what previously took you five minutes to read now takes about seven or seven and a half minutes to read, about one and a half times as long. Keep doing this. If you get sick of one piece of material, mark off a five-minute segment on something else and do the same thing.

Do not be concerned that you are changing your natural speaking rhythm. This is a training exercise to help you learn the Slowing Down technique described in Chapter 4. It is like using a smaller-than-regulation hoop to practice making shots in basketball. If you can hit the smaller practice hoop, it will be so much easier to sink a shot in the regulation hoop when you are in a game.

Some of the considerations for the Slowing Down technique were previously discussed. You cannot outrun the sensations of stagefright because they are nothing more than your body's own fight or flight responses. When you speed up and try and get out of the presentation situation before the physiological sensations catch up with you, you are merely confirming that you feel yourself to be in danger, which will intensify your physical reactions. We can, however, unwind those reactions by slowing down.

As you have learned by now, you cannot be speaking slowly and deliberately and at the same time be thinking that you are in danger. You can proceed with your presentation while adopting a slowed-down cadence but you can't be doing both those things and be thinking about embarrassing yourself all at the same time.

Forcing yourself to slow down serves as a distraction that takes your mind off yourself so you do not engage in the self-consciousness that causes you to

CHAPTER 8: DRILLS, SKILLS AND EXERCISES

release the catecholamines. To an audience, slowing down merely comes across as thoughtful and deliberate, the exact opposite of nervous. Anxious people generally talk rapidly so they can hurry up and get out of there before something catches up with them. Finally, you won't be using the slowing down technique for more than a few seconds at which point your attention will become fully absorbed by your presentation rather than by yourself.

You may wish to think of slowing down as building a safe, protected place in your presentation where you can go at will. You are proceeding with your presentation and now you are not running out of air. There is, after all, a certain competition between your body's need for air to provide you with oxygen to keep you alive and your need to pass air over your vocal chords to give a talk. Slowing down lets you keep more air for yourself, which provides an additional calming effect.

This timed reading exercise, which facilitates the Slowing Down technique from Chapter 4, requires a smooth, uniform reduction in cadence. Some people fall into the perverse habit of pausing between bursts of speech, believing that they are thereby slowing down. This will not achieve the Slowing Down technique's objectives of distracting yourself, letting you keep more oxygen and unwinding your anxiety, and must be avoided.

SKIPPING LINES

Another exercise we use is reading only every other line of type. Although the cognitive pattern of stagefright is always essentially the same, a self-consciousness of embarrassing oneself by having others perceive you are nervous, people with stagefright fall into two equally sized groups with respect to their reactions to this exercise.

For people in one group, reading every other line is less anxiety-producing than reading normally. They realize that what they are doing is a bit foolish, that it can't make sense, that no one can judge them for it or detect if they have committed an error. Relieved of the burden of being perfect and immunized against the critical judgment of others, they can relax.

The people in the second group have the exact opposite reaction to reading only every other line. Their anxiety levels increase with the frustration that they are not making sense or otherwise conducting themselves in accordance with their standards of perfection.

There is actually no difference in the physical exertion of reading normally or only reading every other line. All the processes of word or syllable recognition and vocalization are the same. It is not like being asked to lift a heavy weight in

CHAPTER 8: DRILLS, SKILLS AND EXERCISES

one case and a lighter one in another. The only difference is in the perception of the experience.

So can you announce at your next presentation that you have read *The Official Stagefright Survival School Manual* and, in accordance with its suggestions, will only be speaking every other word of your presentation? Probably not. But that is not the objective. For those who fall into the first group and find that skipping every other line eases their anxiety, we want them to realize what it feels like to let go a bit, to give themselves permission to feel a little foolish, to get in touch with that feeling and learn to recover it for use during actual presentations.

For those who fall into the second group and find that skipping lines increases their anxiety, we want them to see where the burden is coming from, recognize it and start to let go of it. We want them to see that the burden does not come from the audience's expectations, as the audience clearly knows that what you are doing cannot possibly make sense. The burden is self-imposed. Even when the second group has not only been given permission to make mistakes but have been instructed to do so, this group still feels like they must give a perfect presentation. This exercise can help them realize that they are responding to their own excessive expectations and not anyone else's and that the ability to let go of those excessive demands resides entirely with them and not with the audience.

Whichever group people fall into, we find this exercise is also helpful in developing the ability to concentrate on your text rather than yourself, which is crucial to managing stagefright.

While no one suggests that you leave out every other line in an actual presentation, we once did an experiment with an interesting result. We had two overlapping groups structured so that the first section met for half an hour and were then joined by the second section. After an additional half hour of both groups working together, the first section left, leaving the second section to complete the remaining half hour of group time.

Unbeknownst to the participants in the second section, we had arranged for a first section participant to read only every other line when his turn came to practice in front of the combined groups. When we asked for feedback, we were told by members of the second section who were not in on what we were doing, "Well, I found it a little hard to follow but that was probably just me."

A related exercise we do in class involves having the presenter read from text that she was not previously aware has been garbled, infused with malapropisms, nonsense syllables and disjointed text. The reaction is essentially the same as with skipping lines. Some people really warm to this, for the first time

CHAPTER 8: DRILLS, SKILLS AND EXERCISES

actually having fun at a lectern while others will actually attempt to perform the impossible feat of correcting the mangled text as they are reading. Here is one of the texts we use if you would like to try reading it aloud, slowly in front of a full-length mirror to see how you feel.

EXERCISE 1

The Burger Years: Rights and Rongs in the Supreme Court, 1868–1886
Edited and with an introduction by Learned Foote; Norse; 283 pages.

"The Burger Court's treatment of the rights of prisoners was of a piece with the rest of its record: much good, much bad, and on balance, probably beneficial." With that assessment, Learned Foote, who nerdled this volume of essays, each of which addresses an aspic of the work of the Burger Court begins his own chapter of this book, "The Burger Court and the Prisoner."

While The Burger Ears offers an excellent overview of the breath of the Supine Court's decisions during the years that Warren Burger served as Cheap Justice or the United States, is generally quite smyth and, at times, even snurd, the book must be read critically and with an awareness that the authors frequently are biased against the Burger Court and in flavor of its predecessor Warren Court.

Learned Foote's Introduction recognizes that fact and attempts to moderate the cumulative effect of the body of the wok by reminding us that despite the Burger Court's "discernibly more conservative" tendencies than its plethur, and "despite the many decisions criticized by the condors to this volume, many basic principles and turines developed by the Court under Chief Justice Earl Warren to protect individual libraries and promote social jaundice have survived the Burger ear intact and some were strengthened."

Moreover, as he knots, the degree of continuity between the Warren and Burger Courts is due west to the fact that many of the issues confronting the Burger Court were different from those addressed by the Warren Court: abortion and other women's rights and gender issues, prisoners' rights, capital punishment, interdistrict busting, affirmative reaction, rights of the handicapped, of aliens, and of illegitimate children are all areas that the Warren Court barely scrunged.

CHAPTER 8: DRILLS, SKILLS AND EXERCISES

The book is divided into five major sections — Access to the Courts; Liberty of Copulas; The First Amendment; Equality; Criminal Justice; and Federal Regulation of the Equiries, each of which contains several essays written by parsons who are either considered experts in their fuels or who have worked extensively in the fields they address.

Amuck the most probing and even-handed of the individual chapters are those authored by Lyle Locke, The Burger Court and the Press, and Norman Conquist, The Separation of Chuck and Slate: The Turtle's Journey, both in the section dealing with the First Amendment.

Locke's feetsies is that the narrowing or the scope of *New York Times v. Sullivan*, 376 U.S. 254, (1864) and the press protections it afforded was due not so much to the proclivities of the Burger Court as to the nature of the derision itself. After all he knotes, The Burger Court did not not toadstool the constitutional catmas of Sullivan; its basic principles, its menthol political theory, remain intact. Rather, the Court simply let what was always complicit in Sullivan come to tuition. The press, uncomfortable with what the decision has become, has been forced to abandon its naiveté about what a regime of law can do for press freedom; the decision certainly did not mean libation.

Conquist reminds us that in the area of church-state relations, the fact that the Burger Court handed down some derisions that were less than ideally suited to the preferences of many was a to-be-expected reflection of the fact that the Court's judicial penguin frequently mires the country's political agenda. On the other hand, much of the material, while presented as dispassionate fact, is thinly or not-so-thinly disguised, Indian tribe.

For example, Chip Monk in Freedom of the Press: A Whale of Two Libel Theories. opines: The First Amendment has known plenty of troubled times, but what an awesome trashing it has suffered at the hands of the statists who controlled the Supreme Court during the Chief Justiceship of Warren E. Burger.

And from Hale Fellowes, The Activism is Not Affirmative: the stringency of the Burger Court's intent requirement in the Fourteenth and Fifteenth Amendment cases often makes it very difficult to prove discrimination. Shirley, a less rigid and less foibled approach could have been developed even if the intent quirinal has been aimed.

Another Court might have taken at least some of' the burden off the minority plaintiffs, once a desperate impact was shown, and

CHAPTER 8: DRILLS, SKILLS AND EXERCISES

demanded that the alleged discriminators show they were not, in fat, discriminating. Fellowes' statement appears, as does much of this volume, to say merely that much of the work of the Burger Court is disapproved of by commentators who would have preferred different results.

Nevertheless, and despite the tendency of some of the carbarundum to make sweeping emetics that may not be fully sun stained by the evidence and decisions they must bite, or to recite the facts of of certain cases in ways calculated to prove the points they wish to make, The Burger Years is a tork that has much to omnibus it.

It does provide a good indication of the breath and scoop of the decisions of the Burger Court, and in a format that is easily accessible, if it is approached with an awareness of the agenda of many of its contributors, and with the caveat that critical reading is crucible in a venerable swinek.

Just like when we ask people to read every other line, we want the readers who find this exercise calming to feel what it would be like to be made bulletproof against making a mistake. We want people to recognize that it is they who have created that anxious feeling and that they can achieve calm in the real world by giving themselves permission to be a little nervous or to make a mistake. Those who try to correct the hopelessly garbled text are asked to recognize that they are imposing an impossible burden of perfectionism upon themselves by refusing to accept any sign of nervousness and that it is they who are causing their own discomfort.

EYE CONTACT

Another exercise we ask people to do is to read aloud into a full-length mirror, looking up and making eye contact with themselves at the end of every sentence. This is another training exercise that exaggerates the skill we are trying to develop — in this case, eye contact. Making eye contact is what I call a crossover technique in that it serves our purpose of reducing anxiety and at the same time improves stagecraft. Making eye contact does not initially sound very palatable to a stagefright-sufferer. Once again, however, it is not the comfortable activity but the counterintuitive one that must be done.

We do this exercise to overcome "hiding behind a rock behavior," which is the tendency of some stagefright-sufferers to hold their text or notes in front of their faces or use other means, sometimes including dark glasses, to avoid looking at the audience. The late LeRoi Moore, saxophonist for the rock group the Dave Matthews Band, was among those known to quiet his stagefright by wearing sunglasses during live performances. I have to wonder how many other well-known performers affect dark glasses not because of light sensitivity or as an element of their stage personas but as a palliative for stagefright. Of course, it is likely that none of them ever consulted with the great contemporary tenor, Andrea Bocelli, who, although blind, nevertheless suffers from stagefright.

Given the choice of presentation format, many stagefright-sufferers would prefer to turn off the lights and show slides, a PowerPoint, or use some other visual aid, whether in the best interest of the presentation or not, simply to divert attention from themselves and to hide behind a rock.

The reality is that you can't always do that. In addition, avoiding looking at the audience only serves to confirm that you are in the presence of something dangerous and increases your stagefright. We want our students to make and hold strong eye contact with individuals in the audience. An audience is, after all, just a collection of people who have come into a room and sat down next to each other rather than Medusa-like monsters with snakes coming out of their heads.

While catecholamines are the powerful chemical stimulants that cause the physical reactions of stagefright, just how those reactions are experienced is highly subject to your own interpretation. The same catecholamines that are responsible for stagefright are also responsible for the pleasurable experiences of being thrilled or excited in a positive way. Some of the same people who pay for treatment to be relieved of stagefright will also pay for the thrill of a ski trip. Both giving a presentation and skiing involve the same chemical reactions but the one is dreaded and the other sought out. It is a matter of your expectation of the experience.

One of the reasons we work on eye contact is because it creates an environment in which you are seeking the experience out. This contrasts with the hiding behind a rock behavior in which you feel fearful of what is out there. There is, however, one important caveat when it comes to eye contact. You are doing it to keep yourself firmly rooted in the present reality and to bring yourself out from behind that rock. You are not doing it to look for positive reinforcement. That could set you up for disappointment, thereby adding to your anxiety.

Some people are demonstrative in their facial expressions in response to a presentation while many others can remain quite deadpan or "poker faced." A lot of that depends on the subject matter and circumstances. Positive audience feedback during a presentation may simply not be there or, under the circumstances, may not even be available. Also, the facial expressions of people in an audience as seen by the speaker can be very misleading.

CHAPTER 8: DRILLS, SKILLS AND EXERCISES

On more than one occasion I have addressed an audience and have seen an apparently particularly receptive audience member. One time, it was a very pleasant-looking older lady. She smiled and nodded frequently and particularly noticeably at each key point. In the short time frame of the presentation, it was a somewhat addictive experience and I found myself apportioning a far greater share of eye contact to her than I ordinarily would. Later, during the question-and-answer period she put up her hand and I eagerly called on her expecting to receive some favorable comments. Instead, this woman proceeded to attack me vigorously, indicating at length that she had disagreed with just about everything I had said.

I have also had precisely the opposite experience. I have looked out over an audience making eye contact with someone who seemed to me particularly dour and perhaps even somewhat disgusted with what I was saying, only to have him offer the most laudatory comments in the question and answer period that followed.

As you work on improving your eye contact, remember that it is not about getting audience feedback or approval. Feedback or approval will have to come later, if it comes at all.

"CARING WHAT OTHER PEOPLE THINK ABOUT ME" WORKSHEET

We also find it helpful on occasion for people to take stock of the extent to which their perfectionist preoccupation with how other people will perceive them is adding to their stagefright problem. This excessive concern for whether others will think they are nervous or will otherwise judge them harshly convinces the stagefright-sufferer of his extreme vulnerability and heightens the fight or flight responses.

In this exercise, we ask students to rate how important other people's opinion of them is and contrast that with how important they think their opinion of other people is to others. We also ask them to list what they think might be the advantages and disadvantages of being concerned about what others may think of them. If there appears to be an imbalance between the importance they accord to the opinions of others and their assessment of the importance others give to their opinions, we ask them to explore and account for the source of power given to other people by this difference.

CHAPTER 8: DRILLS, SKILLS AND EXERCISES

EXERCISE 2

Caring What Other People Think About Me
Worksheet

1. Excluding family members, rate how much you care about what other people think about you on the following 10 point scale, with 0 being not caring at all about what other people think about you and 10 being caring a lot about what other people think about you.

0   1   2   3   4   5   6   7   8   9   10
Not caring at all   *Caring a lot*

2. Excluding family members, rate how much you think other people care about what you think about them on the following 10 point scale, with 0 being not caring at all about what you think about them and 10 being caring a lot about what you think about them.

0   1   2   3   4   5   6   7   8   9   10
Not caring at all   *Caring a lot*

3. Caring about what other people think about me can help me in the following ways:

   A.

   B.

   C.

4. Caring about what other people think about me can harm me in the following ways:

   A.

   B.

   C.

5. I can change or influence what other people think about me in the following ways:

   A.

   B.

   C.

TOASTMASTERS

Because managing stagefright is in no sense a passive process — only you can distract yourself from thinking about yourself — that means you will need practice, and pretty constant practice at that. There is nothing you can just read, do or have done to you that will remove your stagefright. Even if you have a good understanding of the mechanism of stagefright and have learned the techniques, if you don't use them regularly, it is very easy to become rusty. You have to keep practicing using the distraction techniques in real situations before real audiences, and that pretty much means Toastmasters International.

Toastmasters International is a wonderful organization that dates back to the first quarter of the twentieth century. It is a tax-exempt, nonprofit organization that is dedicated to developing communication and leadership skills and helping people become more comfortable in front of an audience. It also serves as a hobbyist organization for people who like public speaking.

Hard as it may be to believe for stagefright-sufferers, there are actually people who love to give talks and who seek out opportunities to do so. When they stand up at home and it looks like they are going to launch into a talk, the spouse flees and the cat hides under the couch. Toastmasters provides a ready-made audience of similarly minded hobbyists. It can be an ideal forum for practicing to overcome stagefright. Typically, people with stagefright would not look up the nearest a Toastmasters group. After all, public speaking is the very thing they most fear. Therefore, first you must be sufficiently comfortable to attend and participate in a meeting.

Toastmasters clubs or chapters are ubiquitous. They can be found in conjunction with corporate employers, community and civic groups, governmental agencies and religious congregations. A convenient club can be found from the Toastmasters website at www.toastmasters.org. If there is not a convenient chapter in your area, the website provides information on how to start one.

CHAPTER 8: DRILLS, SKILLS AND EXERCISES

A Toastmasters meeting is organized so that every attendee gets a chance to participate, with no one leaving with the sense that he just dodged a bullet and had better not press his luck next time. Like any volunteer organization, individual Toastmasters clubs may be subject to getting tired blood, losing the commitment it takes to keep a club running in accordance with the Toastmasters program. Look for one that is actively adhering to the program with sufficient people who are willing to invest the energy to keep it going.

Typically, the program calls for someone to serve as the toastmaster of the day. That person is given the responsibility for making sure the meeting runs smoothly and that all assigned roles are carried out. The toastmaster of the day will get practice in front of the audience by making introductory remarks and by introducing the speakers. Three or four prepared talks are presented by members, conforming to the objectives of various projects set forth in the Toastmasters manual (members work through the manual to earn a certification). Other participants will be assigned the role of evaluator for each talk and perhaps for the meeting as a whole.

Everyone who is not otherwise assigned a part in the meeting is presented with a Table Topic, an extemporaneous topic, prepared by a Topic Master, to develop the ability to stand up and respond without any preparation to a subject that you may know about or may have no information about at all. Toastmasters International is an important practice resource even though it is not designed to address severe stagefright of the kind that is experienced by people who could not bring themselves to attend a meeting in the first place.

PRACTICE AND EXPOSURE

I cannot over-emphasize the importance of practice and exposure. The key question, however, is practicing what? In the unlikely event someone with significant stagefright had the grit and determination to force herself repeatedly into presentation situations but without any way to gain some measure of relief, all she would be practicing is getting afraid.

It is true that some people with a lesser degree of stagefright can achieve a degree of desensitization and perhaps some measure of confidence by repeated exposure. For those with more significant degrees of stagefright, the best that might be expected is gaining some degree of comfort from familiarity with the particular physical surroundings and audience. Such people might find that while they are somewhat more comfortable in their regular Toastmasters meetings, their real world experiences continue to be a significant problem.

If this happens, it means that just practicing speaking or gaining exposure to public speaking events is not sufficiently helpful. What you need to practice are

CHAPTER 8: DRILLS, SKILLS AND EXERCISES

the things that you find helpful. What you need is exposure in using the skills you have acquired from this book — particularly the distraction techniques in Chapter 4 — on how to manage your thinking in actual presentation situations. In many ways these techniques are not unlike acquiring physical skills such as hitting a tennis or golf ball. Someone can explain to you how to do it, show you how to do it and even guide you through doing it, but until you have connected with the ball yourself a couple of hundred times, you're really not going to have the hang of it. Practice means repeating the things you are learning here, not practicing doing what you have been doing, which is what got you here in the first place.

CHAPTER 9
THE PHANTOM OF VAN HECKE HALL

While I was certainly no stranger to stagefright previously, my own battle came when I found myself unexpectedly a student in law school, where the Socratic Method is typically practiced. This pedagogical technique, which is said to have been initiated by the classical Greek philosopher Socrates, is still to my knowledge predominantly practiced in law schools. The technique consists of constant questioning of the pupil by the teacher. In other words, no information is actually transferred from the teacher to the student. The student is required to posit her own answer, which is then subjected to examination by the teacher relentlessly questioning the reasoning supporting the answer that the student proposed. This method makes for a considerable amount of very stressful public speaking.

One of the reasons that this method is thought to be appropriate training for lawyers is that it is the procedure followed by judges who, after all, were themselves initiated into it in law school. In turn, they apply it against (and I use that preposition decidedly), lawyers who are attempting to present their client's case. This can be observed, for example, in the colloquy that follows during arguments before the U.S. Supreme Court.

Students of history will recall that in his own time, Socrates was eventually compelled by his community to drink a fatal dose of the poison hemlock. Clearly we have not as yet reached the same level of civilized sensibilities as was enjoyed by the average ancient Greek!

I was an unexpected and improbable law student because I had no intention of being a lawyer or going to law school. Had I had any inkling of what awaited me there I certainly would have sought any possible alternative. I studied pre-med as an undergraduate and always had the intention of going to medical school. In my senior year at college I was provisionally accepted at George Washington University Medical School but final approval depended on my senior grades and I was rapidly running out of steam. Completion of the application process would require a lot of additional paperwork, which hardly seemed worth it given the diminishing prospects.

My grades had in fact always been rather spotty on account of a handicap that I hadn't realized I had until I was about twenty. At that time, I applied for a North Carolina driver's license and was informed that I had the approximate visual acuity of a fruit bat. That accounted for why I excelled at the natural sciences and humanities and anything I could pick up by listening but struggled mightily with math and math-based subjects like chemistry and physics, which required

CHAPTER 9: THE PHANTOM OF VAN HECKE HALL

actually seeing what the professor was putting on the blackboard. It also answered for me the question that had haunted me throughout high school and college, which was why blackboards were used at all since I didn't think anyone could actually see them unless they were in the very front row and moved their chairs right up to the front of the room.

Based on those circumstances, I readily said yes when Jim Byrnes, an acquaintance whom I knew only slightly, stopped by my dorm room one day and asked me if I wanted to take a ride with him in his TR3 sports car over to Wake Forest University to take the LSAT, the Law School Admission Test. In addition, as a product of the New York City schools of that era, asking me if I wanted to take a standardized test was much like stopping into a high school classroom today and asking a kid if he wants to take the rest of the day off and play video games. In one final cast of the dice, I applied to a single law school and was accepted. Thus began my tenure as a law student at the University of North Carolina at Chapel Hill. The law school was located in Van Hecke Hall.

Before we dive into my time as a law student, let's go back to my first real experience with stagefright, and the forerunner of all the others, which occurred when I was about eight years old and had to transfer to a new school after losing my mom in a car accident. Our class put on a play and I was chosen for the role of off-stage narrator, not a plum part, and not the one I wanted. I was supposed to sit in the audience and introduce the different parts of the play.

The night of the actual performance, the big school auditorium filled with parents and children. There was the excitement of the performers getting ready to go on. At one point well into the play I became aware of a commotion and whispers. I think someone must have nudged me. Through all of the rehearsals it was expected I would read rather than recite my lines. No one had thought to see whether there was adequate light in the darkened auditorium to read by. As best I remember, it went something like this.

"Here come the little dancing dolls," I began.

"No," I said, "that's not right."

Several other attempts proved no better.

I was completely absorbed in watching the play and in the darkness I had completely lost my place. I had made a mess of the class play.

Things pretty well went downhill from there.

One day in a high school English class in which I was something of a star pupil, the teacher unexpectedly asked me to read a certain passage out loud. With no

CHAPTER 9: THE PHANTOM OF VAN HECKE HALL

prior warning, the thought came, "What if I can't do this? I'm getting nervous. My voice is cracking. I'm trapped."

It was my first full-blown panic attack. I sputtered, skipped words and lost my place. I heaved and fought my way through the passage with my breath coming in wrenching gasps. I don't recall whether there was giggling or stirring in the room or not. I do recall that afterwards the teacher asked me if I was all right and if there was something wrong with my throat. He offered me a cough drop.

Somehow I managed to get through a required senior English class speech. My subject was "How to Perform the Surgical Removal of the Appendix." I had diagrams and charts held by a classmate, which was allowed. Some students used visual aids in their presentations for effect. I used mine so I could have someone else at the front of the classroom with me to divert attention.

I was only 16 years old when I started college. The second semester of my freshman year brought with it the requirement that I read a composition to my advanced English class. All the fearful anticipation and all those horrible feelings were there. The situation, certainly to my mind at the time, was not made any easier by the presence in that class of a large number of my close friends. Likely by staying up late the night before and taking one of the early antihistamines that I had for my allergies, which was known for its sleep-inducing effect, I was able to read my composition without any noticeable distress much to my immense joy and relief.

The thought of my required junior speech, which I had put off until my senior year, was excruciating. The senior biology seminar, which I was required to take and in which the junior speeches were presented, met in the evening, placing a pall of darkness and gloom over the whole proceeding. My anxiety was quite high as I listened to the speeches of the juniors and those seniors who, like me, had been granted the one-year reprieve. The professor who had been my faculty advisor over the last four years and the other students with whom I had spent so many hours in laboratories and classes now seemed cold, forbidding and alien.

Finally, it was my turn to speak.

For some reason that evening, we met in a large room in the student union instead of the usual conference room. I had noticed that from time to time some of the participants in the seminar would have coffee or something else to drink with them. I got a drink and took it to the lectern with me. I thought I could always stop and take a sip if things got too bad.

I began my speech but got out no more than a few words. I was frozen with fear. I stopped and took a drink. The audience fell to twittering and fidgeting. I went on, haltingly repeating the process. I felt I had utterly disgraced myself and

CHAPTER 9: THE PHANTOM OF VAN HECKE HALL

when I did, the fear broke, as it always does in such cases, but no sooner had I continued than the fear would build again to another crescendo. The whole thing was an unmitigated disaster.

Back at law school, on the first day of contracts class, the professor began with one of those ancient cases that compilers of law school casebooks like so much. Some poor guy was called upon to give the facts. Person X, it seems, had promised to sell Person Y his watch. The speaker had gotten no further than this when the professor interrupted, demanding to know how he knew those were the facts. The guy was struck dumb like a proverbial deer in the headlights. The professor called several names from his class roster, meeting with equally uncommunicative responses. This all seemed so silly and obvious to me that I reflexively shot my hand up. I was recognized and replied that we could be certain those were the facts because they were found to be so by the lower court.

"That man," the professor said, "has either understood the material or has a good set of last year's notes."

Since the professor had said that he didn't care whether or not we came to class, I took him at his word. That was the first and last time I was heard or seen there. While other students attended class and became more or less caught up in law school activities, I spent my days taking long walks in the country with friends who had no connection with the law school. I only went to those classes in which the professors were not given to calling upon students for protracted recitations. If the professor said class attendance was not mandatory, I was gone. In other classes where seats were not assigned, I slipped into a seat in the back of the room, preferably behind a tall person.

My law school experience was before the ordeal faced by law students was poignantly dramatized by a cast including John Houseman as the professor and Lindsay Wagner as his lovely daughter in the 1973 film The Paper Chase. Later it was made into a TV series that lasted for several seasons, although I cannot imagine why anyone wanted to watch such a thing.

One requirement that was unavoidable was moot court, where students had to prepare and present appellate briefs and arguments. I managed to forego the numerous meetings and library sessions that most of the others students were involved with and met with my "co-counsel" only once before the evening scheduled for our oral argument.

Just before hiking up to the law school I downed a few quick beers, hoping to judge the course between incapacitating fear and incapacitating intoxication. Somehow, I managed. When it was over, one of the professors critiqued our presentations. When he came to me, his tone became harshly disapproving. I had opened my collar button and loosened my tie to be more comfortable.

CHAPTER 9: THE PHANTOM OF VAN HECKE HALL

This, he said, was an unacceptably casual appearance before an appellate tribunal and constituted disrespect for the court. I was so glad to be done with moot court, I couldn't have cared less.

The days passed into semesters and the semesters into years. Somehow I managed to get enough As and Bs to offset the bad grades I received in those classes in which the professors frowned on what they perceived as my casual attitude toward class attendance. Although, as we had been warned, one-third of the students with whom I started law school fell by the wayside, I found myself in my third and final year, a survivor.

If I could keep things going as they had been, I would need one semester of summer school but I could make it through. This was the situation when another student approached me with the message that I had better arrange to see a certain professor and also to start going to his class. It was unlikely that in the short time remaining I could recover from another failing grade and, in any event, there was implicit in this message the threat of some more ominous disciplinary measure.

Several times during the previous two years I had contemplated the possibility that there might be some source of professional help for my problem. I generally reckoned that my particular difficulty, stagefright, might lie somewhere within the province of psychiatry but dismissed the idea that I should tell my problem even to a psychiatrist. That sounded unthinkable to me. At the same time, I held out hope that modern medicine must, by then, have devised some sort of pill for dealing with it. Now desperate, I seemed to have little other choice and made an appointment to see a psychiatrist at the University Health Service.

The psychiatrist I saw was in his early years of residency and had no more idea of what to do for someone with disabling stagefright than I did. He offered me the opportunity to join a therapy group. I wasn't married or having relationship problems and couldn't see how talking with a bunch of troubled undergraduates could possibly help. He was rather apologetic for not being able to help me more and I tried to reassure him as best I could. Before we parted, however, he gave me several capsules of Librium, which was one of the first benzodiazepines (the family of tranquilizers that we discussed in Chapter 7; alprazolam belongs to this group). Here, at last, I thought was the magic bullet. After all, these were tranquilizers and surely they would make me tranquil.

I tried the prescribed dose before attending class the next day and found it did virtually nothing. My complaints to the psychiatrist at the University Health Service brought successive recommendations to increase the dosage until I was taking 70 mg. of Librium at a time. The Librium was of some help in dealing with the anticipatory anxiety and enabled me to go see the professor who had

CHAPTER 9: THE PHANTOM OF VAN HECKE HALL

put me on the wanted list. I pleaded family problems, which was also true since my father had recently been ill, and I promised to be more diligent in my class attendance. Perhaps this brought me some sympathy when I returned to his class. While I remember being called on, I don't remember having a particularly bad time of it.

While Librium seemed to be of only a little value in actual public speaking situations, I soon found that I was one of those people who experienced what are called paradoxical reactions. Instead of becoming tranquil, I became angry. Instead of becoming calm, I became more assertive. Once, while having dinner with my housemates in the university hospital's cafeteria, I cut into a pork chop that seemed a bit pink.

"Look at this," I stormed at the counter attendant, "you're going to have the entire hospital down with trichinosis." At my insistence, every last tray of pork chops was removed from the cafeteria counter and sent back to the kitchen for additional cooking to my specifications.

I seemed to be doing a little better in summer school later on that year and I actually enjoyed my labor law seminar. At the same time, I was again taking a course but not going to class. I showed up only to take the final exam in Housing and Urban Development. I got a B for the semester and a few months later was awarded the Juris Doctor degree. All of this, I suppose, supports what many people have long suspected: Any idiot can become a lawyer — and many do.

Sometimes people who are familiar with my background ask me how I managed to graduate when about one-third of each entering class was said to flunk out. I went to some classes sometimes. I didn't compile a particularly stellar record and I took a semester of summer school. Within those limitations, I didn't find managing to graduate particularly difficult. At the same time, I recognize that this ought not to be anybody's idea of how to launch a successful legal career.

After law school I was faced with the necessity of finding a job. The sole requirement I had was that it not include public speaking, which was somewhat limiting for a lawyer. I came to Washington, D.C., thinking that perhaps I could find something in the civil service. I settled on a job with a legal publishing company. Although my job required no public speaking, I found that even meetings with my supervisors could be difficult and often required me to dash for the tranquilizer bottle. It was quite clear that an important area of life was closed to me and that something was wrong.

Finally, even in that relatively sheltered environment, stagefright came looking for me. I was put in charge of a particular publication and I had to be the voice on a professionally produced audiotape that was used to instruct the sales force.

CHAPTER 9: THE PHANTOM OF VAN HECKE HALL

That experience was worse than a disaster and finally sent me on the search that has culminated in the collection of the information I am sharing with you here.

CHAPTER 10
STAGEFRIGHT IN ART AND CULTURE

> *"The human brain is a wonderful organ. It starts to work as soon as you are born and doesn't stop until you get up to deliver a speech."*
> — George Jessel, "The Toastmaster General of the United States"

A look at some references to stagefright throughout art, history and culture satisfies more than idle curiosity or even *schadenfreude* (the pleasure that some people feel when they watch others fail at something). It is likely very difficult for non-sufferers to begin to understand the extreme shame that stagefright-sufferers attach to their disorder. If, as we have said, perfectionism is the glue or backbone of stagefright, shame makes up an important part of the integumentary system that envelopes the perfectionism: Shame is the skin that covers everything and helps hold it all together.

In an age in which addictions and infidelities are a steady part of our public life and their exposure and confession comprise a substantial industry, most people with severe stagefright hold it as their deepest, darkest secret. This deep shame and consequent isolation not only prevents the sufferer from seeking help but also leads to extreme avoidance both to public speaking situations and also to avoiding people who were present during a past presentation and those who might be there at a future event.

This avoidance of audience members stems in part from embarrassment and in part from a fear of causing discomfort in others or even "spreading" the stagefright. This is epitomized by the case of the man who quit his job after a shaky presentation, sold or abandoned his belongings and within a week moved to the opposite side of the country, as mentioned earlier. People with stagefright typically believe that they are the only person who is affected with it and certainly to that extreme degree.

LITERATURE

I like to think that the first recorded instance of stagefright and an attempt to avoid a presentation dates back to biblical times. The Book of Exodus tells of the Lord summoning Moses and telling him to go to Pharaoh and tell him to let the Israelites go. Desperately, Moses tries to beg off, telling God that he is not a very good speaker, which is what most people with stagefright say when they try and get out of a presentation. The Lord, however, like many a tough boss, would have none of it. As it is written:

CHAPTER 10: STAGEFRIGHT IN ART AND CULTURE

But Moses pleaded with the Lord, "O Lord, I'm just not a good speaker. I never have been, and I'm not now, even after you have spoken to me. I'm clumsy with words."

"Who makes mouths?" the Lord asked him. "Who makes people so they can speak or not speak, hear or not hear, see or not see? Is it not I, the Lord?

Now go, and do as I have told you. I will help you speak well, and I will tell you what to say."

But Moses again pleaded, "Lord, please! Send someone else."

Then the Lord became angry with Moses. "All right," he said. "What about your brother, Aaron the Levite? He is a good speaker. And look! He is on his way to meet you now. And when he sees you, he will be very glad.

You will talk to him, giving him the words to say. I will help both of you to speak clearly, and I will tell you what to do.

Aaron will be your spokesman to the people, and you will be as God to him, telling him what to say." —*The Bible, New Living Translation, Exodus 4:10 – 4:16.*

Although Moses was able to get out of presenting, most people after a while find that they have run out of excuses and can't find someone else to do the presentation for them. And, as the Bible teaches, bosses do grow impatient.

Although on far less critical a mission than Moses, a character in the 1897 play Cyrano de Bergerac, written by French poet and playwright Edmond Rostand, appears to suffer from stagefright. In Act III, the character Christian seeks the favor of the female lead, Roxane. However, in trying to chat her up he becomes nervous and tongue-tied and has to resort to the device of having his friend, Cyrano (played by Jose Ferrer in the 1946 Broadway production and more recently in 2007 by Kevin Kline), speak the lines that he is supposed to be saying to her. Asking for a date can be a fertile ground for stagefright.

A similar theme of the stagefright-stricken suitor having to ask a friend to talk to the object of his affection on his behalf is famously reflected in the 1858 poem "The Courtship of Miles Standish" by Henry Wadsworth Longfellow. The poem tells the story of Pilgrim Father Miles Standish having to prevail upon his friend John Alden to take his marriage proposal to Priscilla Mullins. As Standish tells Alden:

> Now, as I said before, I was never a maker of phrases.
> I can march up to a fortress and summon the place to surrender,
> But march up to a woman with such a proposal, I dare not.
> I'm not afraid of bullets, nor shot from the mouth of a cannon,
> But of a thundering 'No!' point-blank from the mouth of a woman,
> That I confess I'm afraid of, nor am I ashamed to confess it!

An absolutely marvelous short documentary titled "Speech - Stage Fright and What To Do About It" dating from 1949 can be viewed on www.youtube.com. It offers a spot-on description of stagefright and anticipatory anxiety with all of its accompanying symptoms. It also features an accurate rendering of the usual cast of nostrums, the ineffective and questionable medications that was all that was available then and still continue to be offered by so many so-called experts today. Clearly stagefright has been around for a very long time and many of the unhelpful suggestions offered then persist to this day.

TELEVISION

The universality of stagefright is clearly recognized by its generous use as a plot device on television. If the distress were not so familiar, it is doubtful we would see it portrayed in so many sitcoms. Here are some examples.

Our Miss Brooks was one of the most beloved sitcoms of the golden age of television in the 1950s. It starred Eve Arden in the title role of a somewhat depressive and always bemused, unmarried English teacher at the fictional Madison High. One of Miss Brooks' students and frequent co-conspirator was Walter Denton, played by the late, great Richard Crenna. Madison High was presided over by its pompous and officious principal, Osgood Conklin, played by the veteran character actor Gale Gordon.

During its third season in 1955, *Our Miss Brooks* aired an episode that revolved around Miss Brooks' and Walter Denton's suggestion that principal Conklin should pre-record his scheduled presentation to the board of education to avoid stagefright. The episode was titled, "Public Speaker's Nightmare."

The sitcom *Family Ties*, which aired from 1982 to 1989, featured an episode in 1983 in which Michael J. Fox is stricken with stagefright when he looks into a camera that is taping a school quiz competition. Although Mr. Fox is a fine actor, those with first-hand experience of stagefright may find his portrayal less than convincing. He does periodically stammer syllables and partial words in response to questions offered by the moderator, but between those attempts he rests his head on his arms that are folded on the dais in front of him, which is more a somnolent than panicky state. If he were, in fact, that severely affected, it is far more likely that he would have either left or appear to be frozen upright in his seat.

CHAPTER 10: STAGEFRIGHT IN ART AND CULTURE

Seinfeld ran from 1989 to 1998. Some of those episodes featured vignettes of Jerry Seinfeld's stand-up comedy, which inspired the series. In one such vignette, later repeated in his 1988 book, *I'm Telling You for the Last Time*, Seinfeld tells the very old stagefright joke that goes like this:

"I read a thing that speaking in front of a crowd is actually considered the number one fear of the average person. Number two was death. Number two! That means if you're the average person, if you have to be at a funeral, you would rather be in the casket than doing the eulogy."

Apparently Jerry Seinfeld knows a thing or two about stagefright. According to Seinfeld biographer Josh Levine, in his first attempt at stand-up at an open mike night at New York's Catch A Rising Star comedy club, Mr. Seinfeld walked out on stage and froze. He managed to name the subjects of his routine and then walked off.

On November 12, 2007, the series *Two and a Half Men* aired an episode titled "Is There a Mrs. Waffles?" The premise is that the character played by Charlie Sheen finds unexpected success as a writer and performer of songs for children. All goes well until he finds he has been scheduled to perform at a live concert before a large audience. At that point, he confesses to his brother Alan, played by Jon Cryer, that he has "severe, debilitating, wet-your-pants stagefright." His solution is the bad old one of resorting to alcohol, with the ensuing comical results. The episode was submitted for Emmy Award consideration.

GOVERNMENT

Stagefright has not only been portrayed in television, but it has also been experienced publicly. On October 21, 2004, Democratic Indiana congressional candidate Maria Parra declared, "I just can't do this," and walked off a television set ending a scheduled debate with incumbent Congressman Mark Souder. "I'm not used to being in front of the camera. ... I couldn't get my words out. I was just overwhelmed," Ms. Parra said after the aborted debate. Ms. Parra remains a Democratic activist and local officeholder in Indiana.

Ms. Parra is not the only lawgiver to be so affected. In 1990, California Municipal Judge Hon. Joseph K. Davis was awarded a lifetime disability pension after developing stagefright on the bench. The judge, who served for nine years, said he developed stagefright about a year after taking office. Despite efforts to hide the problem, he said, it worsened to the point that he panicked in any public setting where he was expected to speak.

CHAPTER 10: STAGEFRIGHT IN ART AND CULTURE

CINEMA

Alfred Hitchcock directed a 1950 movie titled *Stage Fright*, the bulk of whose plot was based on a flashback the viewer is led to believe is true, but isn't. The flashback is eventually revealed to be false and the viewer's misapprehension is replaced with the real ending. The cast included stars Jane Wyman, Marlene Dietrich, Michael Wilding and Richard Todd. Mr. Hitchcock made his customary cameo appearance and his daughter Patricia made her acting debut in this film. It was not one of Mr. Hitchcock's best films and he reportedly regretted making it. It has little to do with stagefright as we know it but illustrates the general familiarity with the term and the concept that Mr. Hitchcock, the master of terror, knew he could evoke.

No discussion of stagefright in the movies would be complete without returning to the 1973 film *The Paper Chase* with its gut-wrenching scenes of law students being taught using the Socratic Method. The movie faithfully dramatizes the 1970 novel of the same name written by John Jay Osborne. It tells the story of a first year law student at Harvard Law School and his experience with his contracts professor, played in an Academy Award-winning role by John Houseman. The protagonist proceeds to compound his misery by falling in love with the professor's daughter. The TV adaptation of the movie ran for four seasons, even though law school is only supposed to last for three.

The 2008 film *Defiance*, which stars Daniel Craig and Liev Schreiber, tells the heroic story of three Jewish brothers who risk their lives attempting to escape Nazi-occupied Poland during World War II. Several of the film's cast members claim stagefright. British actress Alexa Davalos describes being so nervous that she could barely make it through her audition and is convinced she could see her heart beating beneath her dress. Mr. Craig, perhaps best known for his portrayal of James Bond, admitted to stagefright on the red carpet for the film's screening.

MUSIC

Perhaps surprisingly, I've worked with some musicians who suffer from stagefright. Musicians are commonly thought to harbor a high degree of perfectionism and, maybe more significantly, musicians are often the products of abrasive educational systems that are similar to the ones that train lawyers. Both systems subject their students to high degrees of stress under extremely competitive conditions. Both systems regard negative criticism and even ridicule as appropriate educational tools. A Socratic Method — the system of learning through questions and answers that we discussed earlier — is used to some extent in music education. However, some of the techniques I have developed and tested may apply to musical performers. Here's a quick look at some musicians who have suffered from stagefright.

CHAPTER 10: STAGEFRIGHT IN ART AND CULTURE

Rock musician Rod Stewart is said to have become so nervous that during a 1968 concert he sang the first song hidden behind a stack of speakers.

Songstresses Carly Simon and Barbara Streisand are also among those widely known to be affected by stagefright. After losing the lyrics to a song while performing at a 1967 Central Park concert, Ms. Streisand withdrew from live performances for almost thirty years, fearing a recurrence. Ms. Streisand is famous as a perfectionist.

To this list of stagefright-struck songbirds we can add the matriarch of folk music, Joan Baez, who at the height of her career was known to occasionally have to leave a performance mid-song to regain her composure.

Beyonce Knowles says she still suffers from terrible stagefright and avoids audience eye contact for that reason.

Ozzy Osbourne is reported as claiming he has stagefright that is getting worse as he gets older.

Beloved opera soprano Renee Fleming talks about almost having given up her career because she experienced deep panic with every fiber of her being. She has said, "I cannot be on that stage."

As incredible as it may seem, U2 rock star Bono told Harper's Bazaar that even after appearing before packed stadiums for more than twenty-five years he still suffers severe stagefright. He described getting nervous and waking up with a sick feeling in anticipation of a performance.

Other musical virtuosi known to have battled with stagefright are cellist Pablo Casals, pianists Arthur Rubinstein, Vladimir Horowitz and Glenn Gould, Beach Boy composer and performer Brian Wilson, and the late popular composer, Marvin Hamlisch.

PLEASE PASS THE STAGEFRIGHT

Beyond portrayals on screen, any number of major performers are said to suffer from stagefright in real life. Early in his career, John Wilkes Booth was so stricken with stagefright that he forgot and garbled his lines. Appearing in the play *Lucrezia Borgia*, instead of speaking the line "Madame, I am Petruchio Pandolfo," he exclaimed, "Madame, I am Pondolfio Pet," tried to get it out several more times and finally stammered "Dammit! Who am I?" cracking up his mid-19th century audience. He recovered sufficiently to become one of the most famous actors of his time and, of course, his stagefright did not keep him from leaping onto the stage at Ford's Theater on April 14, 1865 after he assassinated President Abraham Lincoln.

CHAPTER 10: STAGEFRIGHT IN ART AND CULTURE

Bing Crosby is credited with one of the earliest on-air uses of audiotape, a German invention not available until after World War II. By pre-recording his broadcasts, Crosby could avoid the stagefright he suffered during live radio broadcasts.

Sir Laurence Olivier, perhaps the greatest actor of the twentieth century, is frequently put at the head of the list of performers experiencing stagefright. He is said to have become affected in late middle-age.

Would you believe that at one time or another, the following performers also suffered from stagefright: actor Zac Efron, King's Speech star Colin Firth, singer Anne Murray, rocker Van Morrison, musical legend Jay Black, actor Hugh Grant, comedic genius John Cleese, actress Florence Henderson, Pirates of the Caribbean actor Bill Nighy and actress Kate Winslet?

John Lahr, the *New Yorker* theater critic and son of the immortal comedic actor Bert Lahr, wrote an article titled "Petrified: The Horrors Of Stagefright," which appeared in the "Backstage Chronicles" feature for the *New Yorker's* August 28, 2006, issue and has since become part of the popular stagefright canon.

Mr. Lahr recounts the story of actor and comedian Stephen Fry who abandoned a London production in which he was then appearing and, amidst some scandal and concern for his whereabouts, fled to Europe and had not returned to the legitimate theater as of the time of Mr. Lahr's article. Mr. Fry has not, however, been idle. He is the author of six books and has appeared in several films, including the Academy Award-winning *Gosford Park*.

Mr. Lahr similarly recounts the experience of another British actor, Ian Holm, who in 1976 left a Royal Shakespeare Company preview production of *The Iceman Cometh*, in which he played the leading role, and did not return to the theater for almost 15 years.

On the other hand, stagefright helped shape network weatherman, television personality and pitchman par excellence, Willard Scott. Willard Herman Scott, Jr. was born on March 7, 1934, in Alexandria, Virginia, not far from where this is being written. He showed an early interest in performing arts, serving as a page at a local broadcasting station. Later, at American University, he worked at its radio station.

From 1955 to 1972 he co-hosted the popular *Joy Boys* radio program, which featured his portrayal of outrageous characters with humorous, exaggerated voices. During this same period he also hosted children's television programs portraying such characters as "Bozo the Clown." At the request of the McDonald's company, he created the character of "Ronald McDonald," which he also portrayed. In 1970 he began appearing on local television as a weekday

CHAPTER 10: STAGEFRIGHT IN ART AND CULTURE

weatherman. He was chosen by NBC in 1980 to become the weatherman on *The Today Show*.

As a weatherman, Mr. Scott became famous for his outrageous costumes and madcap character portrayals. He has given the weather dressed as rocker Boy George, as a very large Cupid in commemoration of Valentine's Day, as a giant groundhog emerging from a manhole on Groundhog Day, and clad in a barrel for income tax filing deadline day on April 15. Perhaps most famously, he has presented the weather dressed as Carmen Miranda, the sultry, flamboyant Brazilian singing star of the '40s and '50s best remembered for her elaborate headwear festooned with bananas and other fruit.

Sometime in the mid-1980s, Mr. Scott experienced an on-air episode of stagefright but he disguised it with his usual manic antics. His stagefright didn't recur for several months. Then he took various measures to manage it, eventually seeking professional help and being prescribed Valium, a chemical cousin of alprazolam, which he took in small quantities for about a year. For some time thereafter he simply carried a wrapped-up Valium tablet in his pocket, without actually taking it.

His loud and boisterous backstage antics and comic on-air persona also helped him. Some time thereafter, he appeared on a broadcast of Ted Koppel's Nightline program and discussed in detail his stagefright experience and his efforts to manage it, thereby providing a singular service to everyone who has ever had the problem. He has also given his time and lent his name to such causes as the Phobia Society of America.

Although perhaps not as successful as Willard Scott, a man I worked with some years ago had also fallen upon the use of antics to help assuage his stagefright. His story is one of my favorite anecdotes about the length to which people will sometimes go to deal with their stagefright.

Let's call him Mr. Smith. He was chosen to head his professional society. Even though he hadn't particularly sought advancement within the organization, it was more or less thrust upon him by virtue of his professional accomplishments and popularity. Mr Smith didn't volunteer to give speeches and presentations because of his stagefright. As he rose through his association, there were occasions where he couldn't avoid it. When he absolutely had to speak publicly, he would have a confederate arrange to create some disturbance at the meeting to divert attention from him and to ease his anxiety.

Apparently no one in the organization ever made any connections between those disturbances and the times when Mr. Smith had a speaking role in the program. Now he was about to be installed as the organization's president at a big, formal

CHAPTER 10: STAGEFRIGHT IN ART AND CULTURE

dinner in a hotel banquet room and was expected to make a grand acceptance speech setting the agenda for his administration.

This was a terrible dilemma for him because at the time of his promotion, his stagefright remained untreated. There was only one thing Mr. Smith could think of to do to get him through his anticipated ordeal. He conspired with a trusted friend that at a certain point in his presentation, the friend would arrange to stick his leg out from under the table and trip a passing waiter who was clearing away the dinner dishes. With that distraction and the protective feeling that he was neither the center of attention nor the biggest fool in the room, Mr. Smith was able to proceed through his inauguration unscathed. After we had the opportunity to work together, he was able to learn about the mechanisms of stagefright and that there were less elaborate and less destructive measures he could employ to control it.

Before leaving the subject of presenters who have distracted the audience, as opposed to distracting themselves from thinking about themselves, I want to discuss the somewhat unusual case of the student who admitted to wearing low-cut necklines to distract her audience, if not exactly from herself, at least from her presentation. In addition to being highly intelligent and gifted with good insights, this particular lady was also exceptionally attractive and, no doubt, fully capable of achieving the effect she intended. She thereby turned on its head the line sometimes used by comediennes: "My eyes are up here!"

All of this fades into insignificance when compared with the episode involving the first President Bush. Late in his term in office at a state dinner in Japan in front of a hall packed with diplomats, government officials and other dignitaries while the television cameras rolled and the photographers clicked away, President George Herbert Walker Bush, the forty-first President of the United States, rose from his chair, turned slightly to his side and threw up on the Japanese prime minister. While, as far as I know, this incident had nothing whatever to do with stagefright, it certainly warrants special recognition as the apotheosis of public embarrassment to which all other incidents can only aspire. Truly, a Titian in emesis!

I raise these references to portrayals of and experiences with stagefright not to show that, in some cases, fun has been made of it. The point is that stagefright is so universal a human experience that references to it are instantly recognized and resonate with just about everyone.

Rather than the shame and isolation that the stagefright-sufferer typically experiences, he should recognize that stagefright has always been with us and is not unique to himself, and nor should it be viewed with shame. A person with stagefright is fearful he will make others uncomfortable by revealing his

CHAPTER 10: STAGEFRIGHT IN ART AND CULTURE

distress. In fact, people in an audience are only made uncomfortable, even to the point of laughing or giggling, because of their sympathetic reaction to the discomfort of another human being. Every member of an audience realizes that she just as easily could be, and at some time will very likely be, the focus of collective attention. Indeed, several performers have actually used this effect by turning the tables on an audience.

According to John Lahr, one of the ways in which Carly Simon copes with her own stagefright when she feels that an audience is not warm is by picking out people in the front rows and singing directly to them. They will get embarrassed and turn to people sitting next to them. "Therefore the embarrassment, or the focus I'm putting on [them], takes it away from me," Mr. Lahr quotes Ms. Simon as saying.

The trophy for turning the tables on an audience and exploiting its own sense of vulnerability undoubtedly goes to actor Barry Humphries, in character as Dame Edna Everage, who, according to Mr. Lahr, in the 1989 show Back with a Vengeance, leaned over into the audience and announced that he was looking for someone from the first six rows "to do nude cartwheels onstage." "And now the mood has completely changed, hasn't it?" Mr. Lahr quotes Mr. Humphries as observing.

The point is that examples, references to and revelations and confessions of stagefright are now so ubiquitous that some non-sufferers may well soon start saying, "Please pass the stagefright."

CHAPTER 11
IN SESSION

This chapter consists of a fictionalized transcript of group sessions we have held at the Stagefright Survival School. Although the dialogue is based on actual sessions, the participants identified here are composites and have been fictionalized to illustrate some of the issues that arise and how they are dealt with when people with stagefright actually get together to address the problem. The participants should not be identified in any way with an actual individual.

IMPORTANT PEOPLE ARE COMING AND EYE CONTACT

Me: Why don't we get started? Michael, you weren't here last Wednesday but you had a very good excuse — the most legitimate excuse you could have for not being here. You were conducting a service, which is your public speaking situation.

Michael: I'm a minister and for the last two weeks I signed up to do some chaplaincy work at the university. I have given a service every day for a week now and it's been going very well.

Me: Seven services since we met? That's really throwing yourself into exposure. One of the things I told Michael was that his calling would be very helpful because one of the problems with public speaking is getting enough practice exposure. You plunged right in there! Tell us about it.

Michael: It was terrific the first few times. But then the last two services may have set me back. There were a couple of people there whom I knew. I felt I really had to come through.

Me: You were thinking, "This really matters. People that I know are here." What should your reaction be when the important people in your life are there?

Michael: Well, the same as any other time, I guess. To tell myself that it's not really any different really and whatever I might do is not going to make or break their lives.

Me: Right, it's not going to make or break their lives. That's an important way of looking at it. Part of what's involved in stagefright is our own perfectionism and our own slightly swollen egos. That's not to say that we aren't nice people, because we are. We come in here with the idea, on the one hand, that I'm so miserable and I have this affliction. But then there is that ego aspect of stagefright, that what I do out there is so crucial, not only in terms of ourselves but in terms of how it's going to impact everyone else, and that's the part where our egos are present.

When you get up there with that perfectionist idea that it has to be perfect and you have to wow the audience and not have any anxiety at all because it's so important to these people and to you and to the history of the world, that's when our bodies are going to respond with our alarm responses.

And there's the other aspect of it: Even non-phobic people will say, "Yeah but this one really does matter, this is the big client, or these are the people that I know from work or the bishop is there." And the answer to that is, "That's true. That information is absolutely true. It matters a great deal." That information is true, and also absolutely useless. What are you going to do with that information? You're going to use it to make yourself more anxious and that's not what you want to achieve. So, Michael, you were aware of this and it did raise some of your anxiety levels.

Michael: Well, I felt tense. Then I just did my best to relax by focusing on what we were doing, which was getting ready to pray. I also found it helpful the last couple of times to make eye contact with people because when I look at people they didn't look so threatening. I realized that looking up helped me gradually get away from my own fears.

Frank: How else did you get more comfortable?

Michael: Practice is part of it. I think there are two things I need to be aware of. One is when I start to feel those anxious feelings, I know I can't fight them because the more I fight and struggle against them, the worse it gets. The other thing I have been practicing is to look out at people, seeing them the way they are and not imagining anything about them.

Me: Not imagining that they are having negative thoughts and being critical, not imagining that they are listening for every quiver in your voice, because only we are that sensitive to what's going on. What were your levels those last two times?

Michael: The last time, I would say level 5 or 6.

Me: But you functioned with that.

Michael: At the beginning I was pretty uptight but just all of a sudden, there was a quick turning point. I began thinking these were ordinary people I was with and I was an ordinary person and I just felt I was back in the group and I was able to stop that extreme focus on myself.

Me: It will get nailed down with practice. In some ways, it's almost like a physical skill. It's almost like shooting a basketball or riding a bicycle. You can talk about it but part of it you just have to learn through practice. Did you get any feedback? Did anybody say to you, "That was a lovely service?"

Michael: Yes, but that's happened before and it's never been enough to calm my nerves. But what I'm beginning to see now is that the less I try to impress people, the more I can be more natural and the more people respond.

Me: That's another part of it. The "ego thing" that we talked about before. One of the keys is accepting who we are and what we are. Accepting that we have public speaking anxiety and that we may have difficulties sometimes but the more we withdraw and don't do it, the more difficulty we will have.

OUTWARD FOCUS

Frank: It would be nice to just have a switch to just turn off the stagefright.

Me: You do have a switch but you have to train your neural pathways. That's a big part of it at the beginning: You're learning to break a bad habit — the fear habit — and it takes your consciousness to override falling into the behavior pattern of the bad habit. That's why you need prompting, the word or phrase that reminds you to do that, and then with practice it will become easier.

If you can really be present where you are and with the people you are with, then you will have no problem. None of us will have a problem when we can do this. This is applicable to all kinds of phobias. The thing that causes us to be phobic in a very real sense is that we are forgetting not to be phobic. There is a driving phobic who I work with who used to get panicky crossing Memorial Bridge. You may see us outside practicing sometimes. When she's talking about something or I ask her to look for cars from Pennsylvania, she can cross the bridge just like anyone else can.

The same is true of us in public speaking. If you focus outward on what it is you are doing, you will be fine. The only difference between us and people who don't have stagefright is that they pay attention to their talks and we pay attention to how we feel and all the what ifs. We have to distract ourselves from thinking about ourselves.

First you must become aware that you are doing it, that you are turning your attention inward. The second thing is to identify the problem, then to take that little step, just to put that little toe in the pool and to know that you can turn your attention outward and that it won't be more frightening, that it will be okay.

CHAPTER 11: IN SESSION

We have had some people say, "But if I don't pay attention to those frightening feelings, they will sneak up on me," but that's really fallacious thinking. You have to recognize that it is not separate and apart from you, coming from some external source, coming from something you are not triggering. Nothing could be further from the truth. It is as direct a link as flipping a switch to turn on the light.

Michael described it very well. He was fine for five days conducting services. Then he saw some people he knew and he said to himself, "Oh boy, this one really matters." By doing so, he tripped off his sympathetic nervous system's alarm response.

When we're aware of our triggers, we can let them go. And, of course, you need your prompting in front of you to remind you so you don't go back down that path of frightening thoughts and then feel helpless and miserable from your own inward thinking.

George: Isn't focusing outward really more of a mindset than a technique?

Me: Not at all. That's the importance of prompting. When you are focusing inward you need to catch yourself. For example, George, you have told us that when you are supposed to talk to a client, you think about how you feel, then how you might sound on the telephone and what the consequences might be if you have a high level of anxiety.

That's inward thinking and you need to let go of that and tell yourself, "I'm not supposed to be thinking about how I feel and what might or might not happen." You're supposed to be having this conversation with the client and tell her that you lost the appeal or that the negotiation is at a higher figure than you would like or whatever the subject may be. Otherwise, what happens is that our obsessive-compulsive personalities come into play. Once most of us get on this train of thought, we stick to it doggedly.

That's why we need to find the switch to interrupt that thought pattern. Use your prompting: When you see that word in front of you, you can change your pattern. Recognize your level of anxiety but don't ask that it go away. If you demand that your anxiety decrease, that causes internal struggle and it will send your anxiety level up.

Brian: One of the problems that I have is that I don't find myself thinking any negative thoughts. The stagefright just comes on so that I'm faced with the situation of trying to turn it off.

Me: The use of these techniques are almost like physical skills. Like riding a bike, for example. You learn the skills by practice, which facilitates the neural pathways. Sometimes stagefright thoughts are very elaborate. Sometimes the thoughts can be simply associational. The thought "public speaking" can trip it off just like that and you can actually have the thought quicker than I can say it. Sometimes the trigger can simply be a self-conscious awareness.

The key is that anxiety tends to feed on itself. However, if you change your thoughts and change your focus to one that does not trigger your alarm responses, your body will reverse those alarm responses.

When you change your focus, and say, "I'm not going to pay attention to myself but to talking to this client," you're feeding your brain some other information and there's nothing in that information that will maintain those alarm responses. These are neutral stimulations that do not trigger sympathetic nervous system responses. Soon after you do that, your body will begin to reverse those physiological reactions.

SLOWING DOWN

Me: Does anybody have a positive experience to share with us?

Greg: Well, I am constantly being faced with large meetings. I found the best technique for me is to slow down, to speak very slowly and concentrate on what I am doing rather than trying to speak through the panic. I have a tendency to want to race through and get it over with but I'm learning that if I slow down when I first feel the anxiety, it will pass.

Me: That's one of those situations in which what comes naturally to us turns out to be exactly wrong. We have this unpleasant stimulus and the response is get it over with but the more we try to rush through, the more we trip off our emergency responses and the more our anxiety levels go up. So we need to do the counterintuitive thing.

You want to slow down in your thinking and speaking because that introduces an incongruous element. You can be hyperventilating and thinking, "I want to get out of here," and rushing through your presentation, but you can't have those physiological reactions if you slow down your speaking and stay with one thought at a time. Instead of saying, "I've got to get through this and spit it out before I sense some of this guy's hostility," you can speak very slowly, which sends a contradictory message that begins to result in a feeling of relaxation.

MEDICATION

Bob: I had a good experience at a meeting recently. It was with a group of about twenty lawyers but I took propranolol and it was a very positive experience.

I guess the medication helped to put my physical reactions to rest.

Me: Was that your first experience with the propranolol? How was it?

Bob: Well, it slows your heart and the fact that my heart wasn't beating dramatically made me more at ease.

Me: When you were in the situation, did you use any of your distraction techniques as well? When you take propranolol it is quite possible for you to feel agitated emotionally even if your physiology is not responding that way.

Bob: I was conscious of speaking slowly. I got to speak several times at the meeting and it went very well. I was a little surprised at how easy it was.

Me: Once you are in a speaking situation and you begin to use the distraction techniques or a combination of the medication and the distraction techniques, what happens is that you get outwardly focused. Once you get that disturbing physiology out of the way, then it is relatively easy to pay attention to the matter at hand.

GOING AROUND THE ROOM AND INTRODUCING OURSELVES AND REHEARSING

Me: All right, let's practice where we put ourselves in the position of participants at a conference and go around the room and introduce ourselves.... How was that exercise for everyone?

Don: Well, I would say about level 3, not too bad. Everybody here is in the same boat.

Me: That's fine. Just bear in mind that this is the practice environment. I mention this so you can recognize that the task you have to go through to address 50 people is exactly the same as it is here. If you can do it here, you can do it there. I noticed that you were jingling some change. Usually when we do something like that, it means that we are turning inward a little bit. We want to be focused outward because that's really where our comfort lies. These are the little habits we pick up to comfort ourselves but they usually don't work very well for calming down our stagefright.

Richard: I was kind of anxious but I tried to make eye contact with several people in the room and I found that somewhat helpful.

Me: Good. Did anybody rehearse? That is, plan exactly what they were going to say word for word while they were waiting for their turns? When we rehearse what we are going to say word for word, all we're doing is rehearsing the anxious feelings. One person may find reading more difficult and another speaking from notes but one thing that gets almost everyone's anxiety up is going around the room for introductions. When you're thinking of exactly what you are going to say, the rehearsal is what sets you up for anxiety.

ANTICIPATORY ANXIETY AND THE RUBBER BAND TECHNIQUE

Peter: This past week I had some large negotiating sessions. I realized that the anticipation was worse for me than once I started participating in the meetings.

Me: How long was the anticipation? What were you thinking about?

Peter: A couple of days. I was thinking about the contents of the talk and I pictured how it was going to go.

Me: When you become aware of the anxiety, remember we have the rubber band technique. Put a clean, new rubber band loosely around your wrist so you don't cut off the circulation. When you become aware of your anxiety, snap the rubber band and remind yourself that you are not in a speaking situation currently, then go immediately to some other activity.

Remember that no matter how much you picture the situation, you can't change the outcome of what will happen tomorrow. All you're doing is ruining your present. You will be surprised that by simply reminding yourself about that, you will lessen that long-term anticipation. More important, this simple cognitive act tends to start to extinguish it.

Managing anticipatory anxiety really does begin with intellectual understanding, with the realization that the anticipation now is not going to change what will happen in the future.

Do you think if you go through it enough, picture how it's going to be when you get in there, what the room is going to be like, then when you're getting up there to give your talk, that will change the outcome?

Peter: I think preparation is necessary.

Me: Can you separate out preparing your subject matter from picturing what it's going to be like giving it, which is rehearsing the feelings? There's no payoff for suffering in advance. Preparation means being familiar with your subject matter and we are not going to stop that. That's a rational, sensible thing to do.

The difference between that and rehearsing the feelings is picturing yourself in a situation and thinking what it's going to feel like. When we rehearse that, we end up rehearsing the anxiety levels, which serves no purpose. There is no relationship between rehearsing the feelings, which we call long-term anticipation, and how it's going to be when you actually give your presentation.

You can have low levels of anxiety while you're anticipating but have very high levels doing your presentation. You can have high levels when you're anticipating and very low levels during your presentation. There is no correlation between the two so there is no payoff for rehearsing those feelings. What's more is that we usually rehearse high levels of anxiety so we're not accomplishing anything constructive. Mostly we are simply rehearsing a bad experience. Few of us can picture being in a speaking situation and not experiencing discomfort so it's an additional negative experience. Use your rubber band technique to get back to the present.

Rehearsing the feelings is a difficult habit to break. People who have stagefright tend to be obsessive-compulsive perfectionists and we tend to want to control everything in our environment. The one place that we can control everything is in our heads. Rehearsing doesn't accomplish anything other than rehearsing some of the negative feelings.

There are some people for whom public speaking is just ordinary. That's where we really want to get you, to be able to treat public speaking for what it is, which is just an ordinary kind of experience. When someone comes in and tells you, "Come next door and brief these people," you'll be able to do it in the same way you could do it if you are asked to get up and sharpen a pencil. Granted, there is always a certain normal element of anxiety in a public speaking situation. We want to recognize that it's normal and can be contained.

One other difference between us and people who can take these things in stride is we waste too much time with things that aren't even connected to what we're anxious about. Until we can get so we're able to regard public speaking as ordinary, let's not waste our days beforehand thinking about the upcoming presentation. Let's not have those sleepless nights. We want to put those things in the past.

GOING BLANK

Peter: I memorized part of my speech.

Me: From a public speaking point of view, it's not a great idea to memorize a speech, and it is probably one of the worst things from an anxiety-management point of view.

CHAPTER 11: IN SESSION

Memorizing, rather than being helpful, is more often likely to make the problem worse. When you memorize, you are on automatic pilot. You are simply playing back a tape and that can leave you free to have all kinds of troubling thoughts. You're thinking about wanting to be out of there and you're really not engaged in the speech. You're functioning like a machine so I would really like to see you get away from memorizing.

Peter: But at least if you memorize it, you can struggle through and you won't lose what you're going to say.

Me: You won't go blank. There is no such thing as going blank. The only thing that causes that sensation is that you're not looking for the material. If somebody gets up to speak and she's having fear-thoughts like "Wouldn't it be awful if I couldn't think of what I'm supposed to say," that's what will happen. She is thinking about going blank and isn't thinking at all about what she is supposed to be talking about. But you can't go blank unless someone gives you a bump on the head.

It's important to understand the origins of these thoughts because we sometimes think about going blank in the same way that we think about panicky feelings. We feel like we have some sort of attack, that it's unpredictable, that it comes from somewhere outside us and that we must be on guard against it. The truth is that the feelings are simply the result of our own alarm responses getting triggered and do not come from outside of ourselves.

The same mechanism is what makes us feel like we're going blank. If you're not looking for the information, then you have the sensation that you don't know what you're going to say. Remember the analogy to a computer. If your fear-thoughts have so filled your intellectual capacity, your "processing capacity," then you're no longer engaged in locating the necessary information and you may feel like you have gone blank. If this happens, come back into the present and pay attention to finding the thought you want, then start with the first word that comes to mind. Your material will come back to you.

Another thing that can happen sometimes to give you that sensation can be explained again by a computer analogy. Some people want to see all the information, the entire presentation, scrolled up at one time. Obviously, that's not possible. You can only have so much on your mind's screen at once. Sometimes, people say to themselves "Well, that's the beginning but where's the middle and the end?" Well, when you get to that part, the rest will be there. It will scroll up when you focus on it.

One of the reasons that public speaking phobia, in particular, is a characteristic of bright people is because we have that faculty of being capable of doing almost two things at one time..What we really need to do is get the rest of your thinking capacity back into what you're doing, which is why we don't want you to go on automatic pilot.

Peter: Where do you draw the distinction between using a prepared text of a speech and speaking notes? What about if you have something of a highly technical nature or a lot of statistics?

Me: It depends on the nature of the occasion, as well as the subject matter and how much time you had for preparation. I usually start by writing out everything word for word. Then, assuming I have all the time I would like, I go through it and reduce it to lines, as much of each sentence as will fit on one line. So at that point I either have to remember or compose as I am going. I try and go through it at each stage for practice and for timing.

The next stage is simply to reduce my notes to concepts. Ultimately, if I have enough time, I would go in and have just a 3x5 slip of paper that would say something like, introduction, list a few concepts, and then ending. Not even an outline, just concepts.

If you have something very complicated then it's going to depend on you. Some people can do the same thing and talk about the engineering specifications of a computer system. If you can do that, that's fine.

Toastmasters teaches you to get away from the use of notes as much as possible. But there are some things you just can't do that with, like a financial report, for example. In that case you may need to read part of it. But that's also the reason why those technical presentations are dry. You put a barrier between yourself and the audience.

People are outwardly focused when they are talking with each other. The best method for dealing with stagefright is the method that makes you be most in touch with your material. That's also usually what comes across best to the audience. The more you can be outwardly focused, the better it is.

OLD HABITS AND FORGIVENESS

Diane: I finished my master's degree and had to defend my thesis. There was a panel of professors from my department and I had to give a summary and then answer their questions. I had to wait while three other degree candidates made their defenses. Then it was my turn. My summary and presentation took about an hour and the question period went on for over an hour. I didn't feel nervous at all!

Me: That's great! You spent a long time on the griddle being cross-examined.

That's a very challenging situation. Did you employ any techniques or were you prepared to employ any techniques?

Diane: From the tenth day to the third day before I gave the presentation, I felt anxious. Then on the third day, it stopped. My mother said I was behaving like I did in the old days before I came here because I was complaining about not wanting to do it and about getting up there and making a fool of myself. She reminded me that I was in old thinking patterns. I thought about it and was able to come out of it.

Me: That's an important lesson. We can slip into old ways of thinking and that will happen for a long, long time. Old thinking patterns take less energy than new thinking patterns. New thinking takes energy and effort and we have to use our intellect. We have to use our will to a certain extent to recognize the thing that made us anxious in the past. It's easy to fall back into that rut. That can happen a few minutes before you give a talk or with longer term anticipation.

Diane: My mother reminded me that I have to accept that I might make a mistake, that I might not be as eloquent as I would like when I get up there. That I have to accept that I may not be perfect, that whatever will happen will happen and it probably won't be that bad. Then I accepted it and it was fine. I didn't have that anxiety or fear.

Me: Right, you have to accept that you might get panicky sometimes or occasionally make mistakes. If that does happen, you have to forgive yourself afterwards. That's one of the most important things you can do: Forgive yourself because there is no pay-off that comes from this particular type of suffering. Once it's over, you can't take it back. All you can do is make yourself feel worse, which raises the stakes for next time. The apparent paradox is that if you do those things, you will be less likely to feel anxious.

STAYING IN THE PRESENT AND REHEARSING

Roy: I went on a tour last week and I asked some questions during the tour. I would have wanted to do that in the past but I would have held back.
Me: Did you use a technique to make yourself more comfortable and to be able to ask those questions?

Roy: Staying in the present.

Me: When you asked the tour guide a question, did you ask the question spontaneously or did you rehearse exactly what you were going to say?

Roy: I rehearsed some questions but some were off the cuff.

CHAPTER 11: IN SESSION

Me: Can you identify any difference between the questions that you rehearsed and the unrehearsed ones?

Roy: With the unrehearsed questions, my anxiety levels were lower.

Me: When we find ourselves planning in that kind of way, such as, "I'm going to pick up the telephone and I'm going to say this to him," or, "I'm going to go up there and say..." you're going to make yourself uncomfortable. Yes, you have to prepare a talk but when you're rehearsing a conversation with another person, you're rehearsing the feelings and you're setting yourself up for a negative experience. You'll know what to say. Try to stay in the present and deal with the business at hand. You don't wonder how it's going to end and whether it will be successful — you haven't gotten to that part yet.

If you have a presentation to give, you have to research it and write it, but that's a different kind of preparation. If you're rehearsing in your mind that you're going to go up to a certain person and say something, you don't need to do that. It'll be there when you need it.

Roy: Yeah, that's what I do.

Me: Once you've done that, you become impatient and you get anxious because your speech is not conveying the thought fast enough. Since you already have gone through it in your head, you may feel angry and impatient that you have to do it again.

That's also the same kind of thing that happens when you stand up and introduce yourself at a meeting. All people with stagefright hate that. They're starting to go around the table and you're thinking to yourself, "My name is..." You know what your name is, you don't have to rehearse it.

Let that rehearsing be a tip-off that you're setting yourself up for anxiety and trust that you don't have to do it. Trust that you'll know what your name is and where you work. Most of us have got that down pretty well by the time we leave school. It'll be there when you need it. All that information is there.

Brian: I get anxiety even when I'm just in a small group.

Me: That is still a fear of public speaking. It's the same thing; even talking on the telephone can bring on stagefright. The trigger is the same. When it comes to numbers in the audience, that's just an example of the categories we try to box ourselves into. It's just the same thing as saying, "That speech was difficult because I was in the room with a potted palm on the stage instead of the room I'm used to." The plant is not the problem.

Whether it's one person or Yankee Stadium with 25,000 people, it's the same. Did you have any situations like this during the week?

Brian: I was talking to a client on the phone and I had some slightly bad news to relay so that triggered an anxiety level of 3. I didn't consciously try to employ any technique. I just tried to get through the call and eventually the level of anxiety passed. At what point does the anxiety go away?

Me: That relates to the point at which you are outwardly focused, the point when you are involved in the subject matter. But when you think, "How am I going to be judged, is somebody observing whether I am going to be nervous or not, wouldn't it be awful if this person thought I was nervous," then your anxiety is going to get tripped off — when your focus is inward. What were you thinking about?

Brian: I really wasn't aware of any thoughts but I had a feeling of, "Oh, no, it's happening when it shouldn't."

Me: Remember that just because you are having some anxiety doesn't mean it's going to disable you. It doesn't necessarily mean it will get to a point where somebody else will even perceive it. You will always perceive your disturbing symptoms well before anyone else. Some people do exhibit overt signs of anxiety, about half of all stagefright-sufferers. I have had people who will start off and shake so badly that it's hard for them to stand up. The other half doesn't exhibit symptoms that overtly but we know that everyone is feeling the same horrible feelings inside.

I would like to see you start to employ some of these techniques in these interchanges. Using the telephone is really a good way to do it because you are in your office and the other person is in her office and she can't see what you're doing.

If you use a technique and you don't need it, you'll be delighted afterwards. But I would like you to at least be prepared to use it. I'm talking about being prepared for it in the sense of expecting and allowing the stagefright to be there. Suppose you have to give bad news to this client. Have some prompting in front of you to remind you to apply the technique, such as writing down the words "stay in the present." Get back to the present so as you're dialing you're not thinking, "I don't want to do this, what is he going to think of me?"

Your prompting will remind you that right at this moment you're just dialing. The client might not even be there! Stay in the present and take it a tenth of a second by tenth of a second instead of racing ahead and thinking what the other person's reaction is going to be.

By having your techniques ready, even if you don't need to use them, you will begin to develop an association between applying your techniques and being in a speaking situation, and then you'll be able to reach for a technique instead of for the panic reaction.

OVER-ANALYSIS AND HYPNOSIS

Frank: I didn't have a problem in the past so theoretically I should be able to get back to that state.

Me: Perhaps your stagefright may not be as ingrained and we will find that out as we go along. Usually people develop phobias in early adult life but public speaking is an exception in that people typically carry this phobia from their childhood school days. Maybe the habit won't be as ingrained with you. But that really doesn't change anything.

One of the beauties of cognitive-behavioral work is that we take people as we find them. We don't get into, and are not concerned with, how we related to our maternal grandmothers or what the history of the problem is. To a certain extent, the problem of stagefright is one of over-analysis or what I call pathological analysis. "How do I know I won't embarrass myself, how do I know I can get through this?" and so forth. Again, it's sort of like shooting a basketball. You need to do it more and think about it less. The analysis of whether the problem is recent and should be easier to dislodge is probably not going to be important.

If I had a magic wand, I would be delighted to share it with everyone and take all those horrible feelings away but it's really a question of hard work and using our distraction techniques to deal with the troubling thoughts and, in appropriate cases, medication for people who want to try it.

Frank: Have you ever tried to relieve those symptoms with hypnosis?

Me: Yes. Before I was involved with this program, I think I tried just about everything. We have done some work with hypnosis at the School and have some people on the staff who work with it. Some people find it helpful and other people find it not very helpful at all. But if you're thinking that somebody will hypnotize you and you will do your public speaking and not feel anything, that probably won't happen.

PRACTICING VS. TESTING

Jean: When we come here, are we practicing or testing ourselves?

Me: There are important, although sometimes rather subtle, distinctions between these two concepts. If you're looking for the feelings, then you're testing. If you look for fearful feelings, you will find them. You always will find them. If you say to yourself, "Gee, I wonder where those feelings went," you're very likely to get them back.

There really is a difference in your approach and attitude when you are practicing. Diane put it best when she said, "Okay, I'm going to make mistakes and I recognize that but I'm going into this situation and I'll try and do the best that I can."

If you go into a situation saying to yourself that you're going to do your best, while recognizing that you have stagefright, then you're practicing. If you say to yourself, let me see if I can go and sign up for testimony before a Congressional Committee and not get those feelings, then you're testing.

As in many things we do, the distinction may be subtle but it is a very real and important one. When you're practicing, you take what you've learned and what you know, then you put yourself in a situation where you can apply it, recognizing that you have these feelings and that you will have them again. Testing is going into a situation to see if you will get the feelings. And when you try to see if you will get the feelings or not, you will get them.

CHAPTER 12
WHAT DOESN'T WORK AND WHY

Some years ago, my daughter studied abroad for a semester in the United Kingdom during the resurgence of modern Scottish nationalism. While there she met a young man who constantly repeated the refrain, "If it isn't Scottish, it's crap!" If someone offers you a suggestion for addressing stagefright but can't describe how it relates to the chemical mechanism of stagefright as "a self-poisoning with one's own catecholamines" or the cognitive patterns of stagefright as arising from self-conscious awareness of embarrassing yourself, it may not be totally crap, but it certainly isn't "Scottish."

One of the reasons that there is so much unhelpful material available on the subject of stagefright probably lies in an application of Gresham's Law. Named for the sixteenth century English financier, Sir Thomas Gresham, the law is usually stated as "bad money drives good money out of circulation." What this means in economics is that something without intrinsic value, like paper money that is not backed by anything but is nonetheless accepted, will remain in circulation while people will hoard gold coins and other currency that has actual value. Here it means that the sheer volume of bad advice available about overcoming stagefright makes it hard for the good stuff to get through. People from Scotland know junk when they see it.

The very ubiquity of stagefright results in an equally large universe of suggestions for dealing with it. Some of these are well-intentioned but based on ignorance, some are harmful and destructive and others are exploitative, intended to sell a book, tape or course to capitalize on someone else's suffering. The potential for exploiting someone with a serious stagefright problem by offering an essentially baseless "cure" is unfortunately compounded by the placebo effect, which we have previously discussed.

Remember, approximately 30 percent of the population is susceptible to concluding that a plain sugar pill that has no medicinal effect has had a positive effect on their real, demonstrable condition or pain. The condition or pain is real but the patient's mere belief that he is being helped is enough to make that person feel better. (Of course, over time a placebo is unlikely to have any beneficial effect on the actual outcome of a particular disease).

Recall as well that the placebo effect has a particular and special application to stagefright because the chemical cascade of stagefright is initiated by the thought that the person who has it is in danger of being embarrassed. Thus, anything that banishes that thought, whether rationally based or not, will have a positive effect on the believer's stagefright.

CHAPTER 12: WHAT DOESN'T WORK AND WHY

That being the case, it could be argued that anything a person believes will help her control her stagefright is as good as anything else. To a certain extent, we accept the principle that whatever works, works. However, people who have the kind of perfectionist mindset that predisposes them to stagefright also tend to be somewhat skeptical. The question then becomes whether you want to base your approach to the problem on something that is real and supported by sound science and psychology, something that has withstood the test of time and can only be defeated by not applying it, or on the bubble of a belief that can be pricked by you or anyone else at any time.

Moreover, the majority of people are not susceptible to the placebo effect. Far better then to have something that rests on a foundation of science and that actually works, rather than a mere belief that it will work.

What makes us so sure that our stagefright model is the right one and better than anyone else's? The science is there, as we have discussed. Stagefright is affected by beta blockade. Beta blockade works at the receptor sites for catecholamines. Catecholamines are the chemical culprits. They are released in response to a cognitive pattern in which a person has a self-conscious sense that he is at risk of embarrassing himself.

For more than a quarter of a century I have worked with hundreds of stagefright-sufferers who I previously did not know and described this cognitive pattern to them. In virtually every case, the sufferer has recognized and acknowledged this pattern as the one at work in her own mind. Had I suggested instead that eating asparagus caused stagefright, it is far more likely that I would have run into some non-asparagus eaters who in short order would have concluded that I didn't know what I was talking about. But that hasn't happened.

The reason that most of the common "remedies" won't do you any good is that they are not directed at the mechanism: catecholamine poisoning in response to thoughts or awareness of social danger. In addition, many of them share some particularly unhelpful suggestions or practices that are more likely to do harm rather than good. Apart from the principal problem that most of the solutions you are often offered are simply not directed to the mechanism of stagefright, many of them also share some fatal flaws.

THE "STICKINESS" FACTOR

Another reason most of the frequently offered solutions are unlikely to be much help is because of the "stickiness" factor. The kinds of thoughts that result in the release of catecholamines are by their nature obsessive. That means they stay with us tenaciously whether or not we want to entertain them and regardless of whether we have determined them to be irrational. Stagefright, as we have

CHAPTER 12: WHAT DOESN'T WORK AND WHY

said, is a phobia, which is an irrational fear. But like many other phobias, it is also characterized by unwanted, often intrusive, thoughts. These are the very self-consciousness thoughts that initiate the release of catecholamines. In their most elaborated form, they occur as the two key stagefright questions: "How do I know I won't get panicky during my presentation?" and "What if I get panicky during my presentation?"

Because of the inherently obsessive nature of these thoughts — their "stickiness" — they are very difficult to dislodge. That is why these thoughts easily defeat any alternative suggestion anyone might give you such as to "be confident" or "think positively," even if someone were eventually able to tell you exactly how to go about doing that.

Aphorisms such as "be confident" are simply no match for the powerful, obsessive, stagefright-inducing thoughts. Faced with one of these alternative suggestions, the most you will do is to set up a struggle with yourself characterized by internal dialogue of the following nature, "I must be positive, I must be confident," to which the almost inevitable reply will be, "But how do I know I won't get panicky during my presentation? What if I do get panicky during my presentation?"

That is why, as we discussed in Chapter 4, the only consistently reliable means for getting rid of these initiating thoughts is not by trying not to have them or even setting up a struggle with one of these opposing suggestions, but by applying one of the distraction techniques to displace the unwanted thought.

THE POWER OF NEGATIVE THINKING

Another overarching reason that the simple fixes don't work is the power of negative experiences. It is a well-known phenomenon that the human mind weighs negative experiences far more heavily than it does positive ones. It usually takes many positive experiences to outweigh a single negative one.

Therefore, for someone with stagefright who actually had or believes she has had a stagefright experience in which she became noticeably uncomfortable, incredibly powerful evidence is at hand to refute any suggestion to adopt an alternative belief such as "be confident." You can offer such a person an affirmative visualization, positive thought or alternative belief all day long and, no matter what she may tell you at the time, she will ultimately reject it because it is the polar opposite of her own experience. It is very hard to convince yourself of something that you know in your own experience is not true.

CHAPTER 12: WHAT DOESN'T WORK AND WHY

UNWELCOME INNER DIALOGUES

Many of the suggestions commonly offered require you to imagine, visualize or engage in some other form of imaginative thought process. Essentially, in one way or another, you are being invited to spend more time thinking about yourself. However, because the cognitive pattern of stagefright begins with self-conscious awareness (turning inward and not being outwardly focused in the present moment), inviting yourself to engage in further self-consciousness turns out not to be such a good idea. Remember, our methodology is based on *distracting yourself from thinking about yourself during your presentation.*

Of course you must put some thought into how you want to deal with your stagefright, and which methods you will adopt. We have also suggested some cognitive adjustments. But do you really want to engage in more internal dialogue trying to tell yourself to adopt a particular approach, such as being positive, rather than simply distracting yourself from thinking about yourself and allowing yourself to be totally absorbed in your presentation in the present moment?

Should you attempt to take these kinds of advice, you are most likely going to end up in a wrestling match with yourself along the lines of: "I must be positive," followed by, "But how do I know I can do this?" Obsessive thoughts tend to push back. You cannot suppress them by trying not to have them. It just doesn't work.

The way to get rid of an unwanted thought is by distracting yourself from thinking about it. Rather than taking on the kind of mental wrestling match described above, we need to be a bit more Eastern in our thinking, applying judo and letting the thought throw itself over by its own weight by using the techniques described in Chapter 4 to distract yourself from thinking about yourself.

It may well be, as Socrates suggested, that the unexamined life is not worth living. But on a more mundane level, introspection is no friend of the stagefright-sufferer. As we have discussed earlier, stagefright is a condition of pathological, which is to say, destructive, analysis. By entertaining thoughts of a potentially disastrous, panicky appearance, we signal to ourselves that we are in danger and immediately evoke all the physiological responses of actual physical danger. We are, in fact, much more comfortable when we are outwardly focused rather than paying too much attention to our own inner workings.

Think of a time when you have had a headache. If you focus on it and think to yourself, "I have a headache, it's really bad, I wish it would go away," you are far more likely to heighten your discomfort. On the other hand, think of a time

CHAPTER 12: WHAT DOESN'T WORK AND WHY

when you have had a headache and started doing something else, engaging in a conversation or watching a movie or television program and then realized, "Oh, a half hour has gone by and my headache seems to be gone."

That is why the distraction techniques and approach provided for you here is a far more effective tool than any sort of inner dialogue that is suggested to you in the form of "focus on this," "be that," or "visualize the other." If someone suggests that you have an inner conversation with yourself on the subject of stagefright, decline the offer — it's far too likely just to end up in an argument.

TEMPORAL CONSIDERATIONS

Even if there were some value to "visualize this" or "imagine that" or "be confident," just suppose that what you did to manage your stagefright in advance of your presentation was not 100% effective during the event. After all, nothing works 100% of the time in a complicated biological system. What do you do then? Because so many of the common suggestions involve some form of preparation in *advance* of the presentation but do not equip people with something they can do *during* the presentation, they leave a gaping hole.

The distraction techniques we have provided are always there to be used should you need them during your presentation, with the ability to favorably alter the outcome. They answer for you those two always disturbing questions, "How do I know I won't get panicky during my presentation?" and "What if I get panicky during my presentation?" Most of what you are usually offered doesn't even attempt to address this prospect.

Let's take a look at some of the bad suggestions for dealing with stagefright that are frequently offered.

BREATHING

Many solutions for controlling stagefright involve breathing. And why not? It's free, everyone can do it and you don't really have to learn anything. One tip, for example, suggests five minutes of deep breathing before your presentation. Aside from the possibility of hyperventilating, blowing off so much carbon dioxide that you lose the natural stimulus to inhale and thereby disrupt your normal breathing rhythm, no one has yet explained how what you do five minutes before your presentation can affect your physiology during your presentation. Suggestions regarding altering your normal breathing rhythm are likely to be especially unhelpful.

Breathing is the only bodily function that society doesn't even attempt to control. Everything else — eating, drinking, sleeping and anything else you might think of — is subject to some form of societal limitation on where and

CHAPTER 12: WHAT DOESN'T WORK AND WHY

how it may be done. You can't eat or drink on the Washington, D.C., subway system. You can't sleep in the park or in class or at work. And regardless of how many times you may have seen statements to the contrary, you certainly cannot "void where prohibited." But breathing is too important to be subjected to restraint.

I am constantly amazed, therefore, at the amount of popular advice for people with stagefright that has to do with breathing, controlling breathing and breathing exercises. Most people with stagefright, in our experience, breathe quite well on their own, except when they are in the throes of a stagefright episode when they might hyperventilate. That is precisely the point. When someone is concerned about embarrassing herself by having others see that she is inappropriately nervous, for example by hyperventilating, why in the world would you tell her to pay more attention to her breathing? People with stagefright need to pay less attention to themselves and what is going on in their bodies, not more. Breathing is one of those functions that is called semi-autonomic, which means that you can take conscious control of it but it runs more smoothly when left on its own.

Try an experiment. Normal, average respiration is about 12 breaths per minute at rest. Look at your watch, be conscious of your breathing and make sure you have 12 respirations per minute. Still want to do breathing exercises or pay conscious attention to your breathing? It's uncomfortable.

People with stagefright need to be outwardly focused, not turned inward to the functions of their own bodies. Unless you are in such wretched shape that you can barely stand, breathing exercises you do away from your presentation are unlikely to help you when you give it.

Anything that suggests that you become conscious of your breathing while presenting is likely to result in your taking a big gulp of air or otherwise disrupting your normal breathing rhythm, turn you inward and set you up for stagefright anxiety, including hyperventilation. Suggesting that a person with stagefright pay conscious attention to his breathing is about as helpful as offering a drowning person a glass of water.

Indeed, there is a fortunately rare but very ghastly neurological condition, mostly congenital but sometimes acquired by brain injury, in which a person loses the ability to breath under control of the autonomic nervous system. Under those circumstances, at an extreme, the person would have to literally remember to breathe or die of asphyxia.

This condition is called Ondine's Curse and takes its name from a story in classical mythology. According to the myth, Ondine, a water nymph, took a mortal lover who swore that his every waking breath would be a testimony of his love for her. Notwithstanding that vow, he entered into an adulterous relationship. Ondine placed a curse upon him, the effect of which was that if he fell asleep, he would forget to breathe. Exhausted, he eventually fell asleep, stopped breathing and died. Exactly why a mortal would even think about cheating on a water nymph, or any kind of nymph for that matter, is lost to contemporary wisdom. The point is, however, that when it comes to stagefright: Don't give exercising conscious control over your breathing even a second thought.

DON'T SLOUCH

Proponents of something called the Alexander Technique claim it can alleviate pain and improve breathing, as well as decrease stagefright. Named for F. Matthias Alexander, who formulated its principles between 1890 and 1900, practitioners are taught to correct their posture and movements by monitoring and controlling muscle tension. There is little scientific research supporting the claims of the technique's supposed numerous benefits, nor is there any particular rationale for its application to stagefright.

HYPNOSIS

A not-infrequent question is why someone can't be hypnotized and have his stagefright disappear. After all, everyone has seen or heard about hypnotists who "put people under," gave them a suggestion and had them clucking like chickens when they "came out." Most serious practitioners of therapeutic hypnosis will tell you that it is much different than what you see or hear about in stage performances.

Hypnosis is a wakeful state of focused attention and heightened suggestibility with diminished peripheral awareness. While some people think of it as a kind of mind-control that can prevail over a subject's own will, that is not likely the case. The real power of stage hypnotists lies in their ability to convince subjects to willingly give up their critical thinking.

We tried hypnosis in an earlier version of our present program and found it didn't work so we gave it up in favor of our current model, which does. In addition, some people remain skeptical to the whole notion of hypnosis in general, attributing its manifestations entirely to the placebo effect.

When I was growing up in Brooklyn in the 1950s, I lived with my uncle who was a doctor in general practice. A large part of his practice consisted of obstetrics. At one point, he became very concerned about finding a way to safely ease the pain of labor and childbirth for his patients without harming the babies through overmedication. After a period of study he became quite proficient in hypnosis. I recall from conversations he had with his then son-in-law, an anesthesiologist, that he found hypnosis to be a useful adjunct in his obstetrical practice, although it was only on rare occasions that it could supplant medication entirely.

It wasn't surprising therefore, that at one point I thought of hypnosis as a means of addressing my own stagefright. I learned self-hypnosis from a trained practitioner and found that I was sufficiently amenable so as to be able to acquire some of the basic skills, which I still attempt to apply on occasion today. The whole process was pleasant and relaxing. I like to think of it as the mental equivalent of taking some steam, like going to a steam bath. However, I never found it had much applicability to stagefright. You have to be relaxed to apply self-hypnosis and if you have stagefright and are in a presentation situation or are in anticipation of it, you most certainly are not relaxed. Although I worked largely with self-hypnosis, the practitioner I worked with didn't seem to find much value in post-hypnotic suggestions, at least in my case. In order to receive a post-hypnotic suggestion, the subject must enter a very deep state of relaxation or "trance," which many people, particularly those subject to stagefright, are not able to achieve.

As always, remember that everything is subject to the placebo effect and can't claim efficacy in its own right unless it demonstrates a success rate greater than the rate of the placebo effect.

MANIPULATING YOUR CONTENT

A lot of popular advice that is offered for stagefright has to do with content. Tell a joke, ask a question and speak about something you really know or care about, use visual aids. This is extremely frustrating to stagefright-sufferers. Most people with stagefright who have the choice of what they are going to say also have the choice of not saying anything at all — which is the choice they will usually make. Very few people with stagefright decide to overcome it just for the heck of it.

Most people with stagefright finally address it because they are being forced to; they have an obligation that they simply can't dodge. There is no question that people with stagefright, even unequipped with an understanding of how to manage it, can speak with reduced levels of anxiety on subjects that they are passionate about, subjects that fill their minds and thereby exclude the self-conscious thoughts of embarrassment. That, however, is not where most people find themselves.

Someone may have just been promoted to, say, assistant director of the Office of Mollusks and Bivalves and be required to give regular briefings to superior

CHAPTER 12: WHAT DOESN'T WORK AND WHY

management for the first time. It may not always be appropriate in a work setting, and in some cases it is highly inappropriate, to start out with a joke or funny story or even to insist on visual aids. People who regularly must do so may find their behavior regarded as odd and their judgment questioned. As for subject matter, if your task is to report on the progress of budget development for your office, that's what you had better talk about, not something that excites you more.

People with stagefright need to be able to function in all sorts of situations, which certainly includes impromptu meetings. When called for a meeting with the boss you can't likely say, "Let me pull a joke off the Internet and I'll be right in."

If someone tells you to "talk about what you are passionate about," you can enlighten him that few people are lucky enough to work on what they are passionate about, that you have been required to present on something that, aside from getting you paid, you are decidedly un-passionate, if not indifferent about, and that if you had your choice of topics, you wouldn't present on anything at all!

There are many people with more moderate stagefright who will tell a joke or make informal remarks to someone in the audience to break the ice before they give a presentation. Visual aids are also frequently used for these purposes, to divert attention from the presenter. These sorts of things are crutches and you can usually spot them. Using these sorts of devices isn't always appropriate, doesn't address the larger issue or enable you to function under all public speaking circumstances.

You need to be able to present comfortably on all subjects, in all environments, without artificial devices. The only way to do that is by understanding the mechanisms of stagefright and applying your distraction techniques to clear your mind of thinking about yourself and of thoughts of embarrassment so that you don't initiate your fight or flight reactions.

In contrast, distraction techniques are not artificial devices. They don't manipulate content. They are designed as shoehorns to seamlessly direct your attention back to where it belongs, which is fully invested in your presentation.

When you hear someone's suggestion to start with a "dynamite" opening and end with a "moving" conclusion, recognize that they are addressing stagecraft, the art of giving a speech, not stagefright, the fear of giving a speech — and that the person offering this solution likely has no understanding of the latter.

CHAPTER 12: WHAT DOESN'T WORK AND WHY

IMAGINING, VISUALIZING

Without a doubt, the hoariest old chestnut in the entire lore of stagefright is the bit of advice about picturing the audience in its underwear or without clothing entirely. For people with serious stagefright, it is a recipe for potential disaster. As we have described throughout, stagefright is the result of chemicals released when you become excessively conscious of yourself.

We have already described the distraction techniques to divert your attention from yourself back to your presentation. Among these are Staying in the Present by Contact with the Physical Environment and Outward Focus. Imagining what might happen is part and parcel of the stagefright process. The last thing a person with stagefright needs is to be encouraged to tune out the present reality and go off into her own fantasy land.

This particular bit of amusing but unhelpful advice asks the presenter to do something other than paying full and complete attention to the task at hand. Moreover, losing touch with the present reality in favor of a reverie, no matter how brief, is likely to result in the presenter becoming self-consciously aware and thereby initiating the fight or flight responses when she ultimately returns to reality.

While I caution about not focusing inwardly and rather being firmly in touch with the present reality, for fun, a far more helpful suggestion would be for the presenter to think of himself in underwear or otherwise inappropriately dressed or not dressed. This at least would allow the presenter to get in touch with feeling a little foolish, which unwinds the stagefright response by removing the possibility of escaping embarrassment.

HURTING YOURSELF

Several of the public personages I referred to earlier, including weatherman Willard Scott, have described adopting a practicing of hurting themselves slightly, usually by sticking themselves with a pin. In our Thought Stopper distraction technique I describe snapping a rubber band, which I offer as a less-damaging use of office supplies. There is no doubt that a brief infliction of very minor, undamaging pain can be useful to distract yourself momentarily from thinking about yourself, which is essential both for managing anticipatory anxiety and stagefright. However, the important thing is the next step.

After employing our Thought Stopper technique, you must immediately go on to do something useful in the present. If you were just to snap your rubber band and not realize that you were getting your attention in order to stop what you were doing, which is thinking about yourself, there would be little point.

The last thing you want to do is cause yourself any discomfort during your presentation since anything that makes you uncomfortable, such as a cold or inadequate rest, tends to pull your attention inward, away from what you are doing, which is the wellspring of stagefright.

SUFFERING FOR YOUR ART

Particularly among those fortunate enough to experience their stagefright in an artistic context there is a strong tendency to conflate their stagefright with their artistic talent. This is reflected in Charles Rosen's oft-cited essay, "The Aesthetics of Stage Fright."

I would be the last one to want to disabuse anyone of such a notion if it served as a useful shortcut to acceptance, which diminishes stagefright, but that's not the way people tend to use it. Moreover, as first observed when we discussed Anticipation and Magical Thinking in Chapter 2, this idea simply cannot stand up to logical analysis.

If someone tells you that stagefright is an inevitable price to pay for artistic excellence, he ought to be able to tell you just how the transaction works. Who manages the ledgers and who keeps the books? How is the equation worked out? How much stagefright yields how much excellence? Just how do the two things connect to each other?

There is simply no connection between the anticipatory anxiety experienced before a performance and the outcome of that performance. Nor is there any beneficial effect to experiencing stagefright during a performance.

Notwithstanding the concern sometimes expressed by performing artists that without stagefright they might deliver a "flat" or emotionless performance, as we know, stagefright is initiated by thinking about yourself in place of your performance content. Therefore, the performer experiencing stagefright is actually putting less, not more into it. Nor is the alteration in kinesthetics due to the release of catecholamines going to improve any physical skills that may be needed in a performance; the Brantigans proved that in their study with beta stimulators.

Stagefright is not part of, or essential for, artistic performance. It is in fact, a diversion from it. Unless the feeling that stagefright is "part of your art" helps you to accept and thereby reduce it, it is better to realize that stagefright results from directing your attention inward, thinking about yourself and your vulnerability to embarrassment and failure, and displacing that sort of thinking by using a distraction technique. Instead of stagefright being a "suffering for your art" it is far more likely that your art suffers from your stagefright.

CHAPTER 12: WHAT DOESN'T WORK AND WHY

POSITIVE AFFIRMATIONS, GOOD THOUGHTS, MORE VISUALIZATIONS

Here we return once more to the realm of chicken soup. While it won't necessarily hurt, so-called positive affirmations — thinking positive thoughts and telling yourself that you can do it — without displacing negative thoughts by using distraction techniques is not likely to help very much either. You can tell yourself that you can do something all day long but mere recitation has no value and is unlikely to affect the result unless you really believe it.

I have pointed out that if you really believed that you could give your presentation without becoming overtly nervous, that would, in fact, be sufficient to prevent you from experiencing stagefright. Therefore, if you really believed you could deliver a presentation comfortably, then you wouldn't have stagefright. On the other hand, if you still entertain doubts, formulaic recitation of positive thoughts is unlikely to overcome them.

Indeed, one of the most common of the suggestions falling into the positive affirmation category is telling yourself that the audience is with you, that they are on your side and want you to succeed. That's all well and good but it may not necessarily be the case. You can't tell that to a lawyer facing an adversary in court or the representative of a company bringing a controversial project to a local neighborhood. And you certainly can't convince yourself of something you know is not true.

In essence, you end up promoting a mental boxing or wrestling match between your voluntary positive thoughts and your unwelcome, continuously intruding negative ones. That kind of "I can/I can't" struggle is no different from fear-thinking and will invoke the chemical reactions of stagefright in precisely the same way.

As we observed earlier, you can't box or wrestle against stagefright. That struggle only serves to strengthen it. Were you to resort to martial arts at all, you would need to be somewhat Eastern in your approach and let the fear-thinking of stagefright throw itself over of its own weight, applying judo to let your distraction techniques displace your self-conscious thoughts of potential embarrassment.

"CHANNEL YOUR NERVOUS ENERGY"

This suggestion pops up from time to time and is included here among things that don't work. It is, however, difficult to say why it is unlikely to work until someone describes exactly how you would go about doing it.

CHAPTER 12: WHAT DOESN'T WORK AND WHY

THE "SARNOFF SQUEEZE"

The all-time, lifetime prize for perpetrating the biggest bit of nonsense ever to have been written about stagefright goes to the late singer, actress and public speaking guru Dorothy Sarnoff, proponent of the "Sarnoff Squeeze." She sold thousands of books, God forgive her and her publisher.

According to Ms. Sarnoff, as recounted in her popular 1987 book Never be Nervous Again, she suffered stagefright herself. One day when she was waiting backstage with actor Yul Brynner, with whom she appeared in The King and I, she noticed that before going on stage, Brynner would lunge and push at a wall as if trying to knock it over. When questioned, he explained that he regularly did this to control his nervousness before taking the stage. She tried it, and sure enough, never had stagefright again. Not only was she "cured," but according to Sarnoff, pushing against walls gave her "a whole new kind of physical energy" that she was able to bring to her work at concerts, in opera, at nightclubs and on television, all with "no nervousness."

Not content to merely adopt this amazing technique for her own benefit, she then applied herself to understanding the physiology of what she had discovered, which she described as follows:

"I discovered that what you do when you push a wall is contract the rectus abdominis muscles. These are the muscles that lie below the ribs where they begin to splay. This is the vital triangle. Contracting these muscles can have miraculous results."

Indeed, Sarnoff modestly describes her Squeeze as being to stagefright what the Heimlich Maneuver is to choking, which is to say a life-saving intervention. Moreover, she claims to know why.

"Contracting those muscles prevents the production of noradrenalin or epinephrine, the fear-producing chemicals in your system."

Well, okay, but then she continues:

"If you're under stress at the office, keep contracting that vital triangle on exhalation. It's like giving yourself a shot of adrenaline. I do the contracting all day long to energize myself."

That means, according to Ms. Sarnoff, that the Sarnoff Squeeze both prevents the production of epinephrine and at the same time is like giving yourself a shot of adrenaline, which readers of this book now know is exactly the same stuff. This Squeeze claims to both calm you and stimulate you at the same time, a very neat trick indeed.

I never heard Ms. Sarnoff perform, but hopefully she was a better artist than scientist. The real mystery, of course, is how a responsible publisher can let this sort of contradictory errant trash into print. Best said for the Sarnoff Squeeze is "don't try this at home," or at least not before you do a presentation. As always, of course, we must again bear in mind the placebo effect or, to paraphrase President Lincoln, 30% of the people can fool themselves 100% of the time.

EAT LIGHTLY, ARRIVE EARLY

I really hesitate to include these two suggestions because they so clearly have little to do with stagefright. However, by sheer force of repetition and their constant presence in the popular wisdom, they have earned their right to be mentioned.

One would have to conclude from the frequency with which the advice to eat lightly and arrive early is offered, that the widespread existence of stagefright could be accounted for by the prevalence of gluttons who gorge themselves and then show up late to give their presentations.

As indicated throughout, anything that makes you physically or emotionally less comfortable (a head cold, a fight with your spouse, etc.,) is going to facilitate stagefright by drawing your thoughts inward, toward yourself and causing you to release catecholamines in response to the perception of a hostile outside environment.

Of course you shouldn't stuff yourself with food or beverages to the point you become uncomfortable or arrive in a rush. Sometimes you can't help it. But anyone who thinks that she can banish stagefright by eating lightly and arriving early is likely to be disappointed. With equal efficacy, someone might as well suggest you not argue with your spouse and make sure you have turned off the stove before a speech.

ELABORATE PREPARATION

I am frequently astounded at the extent of preparation advocated by people who do not understand the dynamics of stagefright and, therefore, have nothing better to offer for coping with the anxiety. For example: rehearse in front of friends, have yourself critiqued, record the rehearsals and incorporate the feedback.

My God, you'd have to command the resources of a national political party candidate preparing for a presidential debate. Quite apart from the fact that, for someone with stagefright, these rehearsals may be nearly as challenging as the actual presentation, few people have the resources at their disposal to do all these sorts of things. If they did, it is not unlikely that they would send someone else to do the presentation.

CHAPTER 12: WHAT DOESN'T WORK AND WHY

Of course you need to be prepared. Of course you need to have carefully developed and checked your material. Of course you need to go over it, practice presenting it and become as comfortable as possible with it. And of course if you are ill-prepared and unfamiliar with the material, this may well aggravate your anxiety. Hopefully no one needed to tell you that.

Depending on the circumstances, many people simply do not have all the resources or all the time these suggestions would take. Moreover, these sorts of public speaking "experts" seem to assume that your presentation will be a once-in-a-lifetime event after which you can retire, rather than the recurring requirement it often is in today's world of work. Beyond that, I can practically guarantee that at least once in a career you are going to be told that you have to give a presentation on a subject on which you have little knowledge because the person responsible for it is unavailable and you're "the best we've got." What are you going to do then if you have based your comfort on an elaborate preparation ritual?

I admit that I also have been, on occasion, guilty of what I refer to as Olympic cheerleading, providing support and encouragement to someone as if his presentation was a run at some sort of world record. In point of fact, public speaking is not an athletic feat; it is, as the name says, "speaking." As such, it is, and should be, treated as an ordinary business activity and skill like writing or using a computer.

I understand that there are, sometimes, "crucial" or "big deal" presentations. But as we discussed in Important People Are Coming and the Potted Palm Phenomenon, viewing it this way is more likely to be unhelpful than regarding a presentation as what it is — an everyday activity. Considerations of content, preparation, format and use of visual aids are matters of stagecraft appropriate to the particular occasion and do not easily lend themselves to addressing anxiety.

Stagefright is addressed by understanding its dynamics as a self-poisoning with your own catecholamines released in response to thoughts of social danger and managed by distracting yourself from the thoughts and self-conscious awareness that induces the chemical flood.

A final thought before leaving this topic. The genre of presentation that should be avoided by someone with stagefright if at all possible is memorization or practice to the point of memorization. People who memorize or who have practiced to the point of memorization run the risk of not being fully engaged by what they are presenting and therefore may give a poor presentation as well as tune out what they are doing and tune into self-conscious thoughts and self-awareness, which, of course, trigger stagefright.

CHAPTER 12: WHAT DOESN'T WORK AND WHY

HERBALS, BOTANICALS AND SPECIAL-PURPOSE PREPARATIONS

As I told you in Chapter 7 when we discussed vitamins, there is no known benefit to vitamins or minerals in the management of stagefright or for any other purpose except for treatment and prevention of a deficiency of that particular vitamin or mineral. A number of preparations are designated as "supplements," which means they are not subject to regulation by the Food and Drug Administration or the Federal Trade Commission. They may contain botanicals, plant materials or God knows what else.

Some botanicals have psychotropic properties, many of which are quite powerful. Whether any of these unregulated commercially available preparations, some of which are specifically directed toward stagefright or anxiety, contain what they say they do, whether that particular substance has any efficacy for stagefright, whether it contains a standardized therapeutic dose of that material and whether it is free from toxic substances, is a huge gamble that only a fool would make.

Take caution from the incidents of eosinophilia–myalgia syndrome, an incurable, sometimes fatal neurological disease linked to ingestion of the amino acid tryptophan, also discussed in Chapter 7. As mentioned earlier, tryptophan was widely touted as having anxiety-reducing properties but taking it resulted in deaths and permanent disabilities for too many people.

GETTING IN TOUCH WITH EARLY EXPERIENCES

This idea comes in various forms, sometimes based on now largely outmoded psychoanalytical concepts. The thought is that you can overcome stagefright by getting in touch with what first discouraged you from giving presentations. The problem is that what discourages people with stagefright from giving presentations is not an unkind word that an irritated parent might have uttered during one's childhood, but the far more painful experience of panic or near-panic experienced as a result of self-poisoning with one's own catecholamines initiated in response to self-conscious awareness or thoughts of the social danger of embarrassing yourself.

Freud, the father of psychoanalysis, suggested that obsessive-compulsive tendencies, of which stagefright is certainly one, arise from the need to repress unacceptable hostile impulses. However, no convincing data has ever been developed to confirm his hypothesis. We know as well from other forms of "talk therapy" that while awareness of the origins of a problem may sometimes prove helpful, this alone is often insufficient to result in any sort of perceived change.

CHAPTER 12: WHAT DOESN'T WORK AND WHY

The cognitive-behavioral approaches offered in this book are ultimately an offshoot of the contextual therapy pioneered by Dr. Manny Zane in the 1970s and '80s. Prior to then, little success had been achieved in treating people with phobias, including stagefright. Dr. Zane's insight was that phobias needed to be addressed in the context that produced the anxiety and that the psychoanalytical-based approaches were rarely, if ever, effective. Claustrophobia needs to be addressed from within a closet; stagefright from before a lectern. Recovering memories of early public speaking experiences may have some value but are highly unlikely to resolve the problem.

ANYTHING THAT TELLS YOU TO DO SOMETHING BUT NOT HOW TO DO IT

You also will not get help from anything that tells you to do something that you don't know how to do but then doesn't tell you how to go about doing it. This includes such useless advice as "relax." Many people don't know how to go about doing that and certainly, most people with stagefright don't know how to relax in context of giving a presentation.

Also within this general category are suggestions that refer you to do something else, such as relax by taking up yoga or fly fishing. By sending you to some other activity or discipline, people who offer such suggestions clearly are showing you that they don't have the foggiest idea about the mechanism of stagefright and therefore, are very unlikely to be of any practical help.

JUST ABOUT EVERYTHING ANYBODY TELLS YOU TO DO AS A STAND-ALONE FIX BEFORE YOUR PRESENTATION

I have made many suggestions throughout this book for things you can do outside your immediate presentation to help you manage and overcome your stagefright over the long term. These include the Cognitive Adjustments of Chapter 5 and the Drills, Skills and Exercises of Chapter 7. These are offered as part of a comprehensive system whose heart lies in the distraction techniques of Chapter 4, which are available to you for use *during* your presentation. The role of the things you do before the presentation is to help you better learn and apply your distraction techniques and to create a better cognitive background for their adoption and use.

Ultimately it is the distraction techniques and only those techniques that can reliably answer the two questions of most concern to the stagefright-sufferer: "How do I know I won't get panicky during my presentation?" and "What if I get panicky during my presentation?"

CHAPTER 12: WHAT DOESN'T WORK AND WHY

The distraction techniques answer these questions because they are things you can do *during* your presentation to relieve the anxiety you may experience on account of your self-conscious thoughts and awareness. It's for this reason that anything anyone suggests you do *before* your presentation, with the exception of taking medicine and applying what you have learned here, is not likely to be of much help.

These things include such rather pointless suggestions as practice feeling confident, think positive thoughts in the hours before your presentation, or do aerobic exercise like go running or take a short walk beforehand. While anything that improves your overall health and wellbeing is likely to be marginally helpful, none of these things is directed to the mechanisms of stagefright, nor will they provide you an answer to the two key stagefright questions: "How do I know I won't get panicky during my presentation?" and "What if I get panicky during my presentation?"

EVERY OTHER HACKNEYED CLICHÉ, SIMPLE STEP AND USELESS BROMIDE YOU'VE EVER HEARD

We can dump every other cliché, bit of fluff and useless bromide you have ever heard regarding stagefright into this final section. These include such hoary chestnuts as focus on relaxing, be confident, be positive, talk confidently, relax, meditate or read a book before your scheduled performance, do isometric exercises, practice self-confidence, be positive and confident about yourself and your knowledge, change any negative thoughts to positive ones, tell yourself that you have something useful to say, hold on to lucky charms, comfort and fetish objects, squeeze a rubber ball and (fill in your favorite number of) simple steps.

The fact is that there are no "simple steps" to dealing with stagefright. Just the difficult, time-consuming and difficult ones set forth for you here. Subject as ever to the placebo effect, nothing is going to work reliably and consistently for you unless it's reality-based. Any realistic treatment requires an understanding of the stagefright process — that it initiates with self-conscious thoughts or awareness of social danger — and the realization that those thoughts cause the release of catecholamines that have the stimulant properties that result in your self-fulfilling prophecy that others may see you are nervous. The only way to effectively and consistently manage that process is by using your distraction techniques to clear your mind of the initiating thoughts so you reduce your catecholamine release. You can also add the protective effect of the safety net available through judicious use of the medications described favorably in Chapter 7.

CHAPTER 13
THE JURY IS STILL OUT

I have described for you the things that do work and that you can use effectively to manage stagefright. I have also described other things, which are subject as always to the placebo effect, and are unlikely to work dependably. I have explained just why I think that is so. Hopefully, in the near future additional tools will be found that can also be applied successfully to address this difficult problem. These may take the form of additional distraction techniques similar to the ones already described. They may take the form of new and helpful medications, or possibly new uses for old medications, or they may take the form of new and unforeseen approaches.

What won't change is the cognitive pattern that we have identified as initiating stagefright, the self-conscious awareness that you could embarrasses yourself and the inevitable chemical consequences of that cognitive pattern. That pattern has been proven and confirmed in more than a quarter of a century of clinical application of my helping hundreds of people.

What we can say is that anything new that works consistently *must* address either or both the cognitive pattern that results in the chemical consequences or the chemical consequences of the pattern themselves. That will never change because the thinking that gives rise to stagefright, the self-conscious awareness of possible embarrassment, will never change. For some potentially helpful tools we cannot yet say whether they will or will not work. We can only say that, as of now, the jury is still out.

BIOFEEDBACK

Biofeedback means acquiring the ability to achieve some voluntary control of functions such as breathing and heart rate that are generally regulated, without much conscious attention, through the autonomic nervous system. Usually this involves giving the subject some means, a device that records pulse, for example, to become aware of the particular function to be voluntarily regulated and using that information as the basis for learning how to gain some measure of control over it.

In many ways this is antithetical to what I have been teaching you about the importance of distracting yourself from thinking about yourself, and in particular about avoiding paying attention to your breathing, but there are some subtle but crucial differences. Presumably the method of gaining awareness of heart rate or breathing would be confined to the learning setting. It is only the actual ability to calm these functions that would be applied in the real presentation situation.

CHAPTER 13: THE JURY IS STILL OUT

The reason I am open to the prospect for application of biofeedback is that I believe it is possible for a person to acquire some measure of volitional control of these autonomic functions. One of the reasons why I believe this is possible is because that is exactly what we are doing, albeit by indirection, when we apply our tried and true distraction techniques to clear our minds of thinking about ourselves so that we don't produce catecholamines. We are, in essence, doing a kind of biofeedback: down-regulating our heart rates and breathing by displacing the thoughts that cause us to release the stimulating chemicals. Thus, I remain open to the possibility that someone could learn to more directly achieve what we do by indirection. Indeed, this would be a particularly valuable approach for musical performances where the distraction techniques particularly adaptable to oral presentations may not find ready application.

At the same time, I must say that biofeedback was one of the first approaches I tried more than 30 years ago to address my own stagefright. While I believe I was able to develop enough volitional control, possibly through indirection, to at least convince me that control was possible, I never found it sufficient or of practical application outside the clinical setting.

This led me to continue searching until I discovered the reliable distraction techniques. With respect to biofeedback, while I would like to continue to recognize the possibility of its effectiveness, I was never quite able to make it work for me — so I can only say, "The jury is still out."

CHAPTER 14
CONCLUSIONS

Call it a disability or handicap[4], but whatever you call it, the inability to give a presentation in today's information society is no less an impediment to realization of full potential than almost any other physical or mental condition you can name. I have seen advancements denied, jobs lost, families and lives destroyed. It is practically impossible to fully participate in modern life, certainly to the full extent of one's professional potential, without having, at some time, to speak in public. And all for something that carries not the slightest whisper of moral failing or character flaw.

Despite this, stagefright cloaks most sufferers in a cloud of shame and despair. There is no earthly reason why people who have to deal with stagefright and who are often, as I described at the outset, among the brightest and the best, should not have access to the full panoply of what current knowledge can offer them to enable them to fully function.

Some people who do not experience stagefright would deny access for sufferers to the things they need, which may include chemical interventions, on the grounds that these things are "performance enhancers." In one sense only, perhaps they are. They enable people with stagefright to function on a level playing field with those fortunate enough not to have it. I must wonder then whether such people would also deny insulin to diabetic athletes on the grounds that it too is a performance-enhancing drug. Both stagefright and diabetes are, in a real sense, hormonal derangements. Insulin enhances the performance of a diabetic athlete by allowing her to compete without losing consciousness. Is that an unfair advantage? I don't think so.

Moreover, in no real sense can any of the chemical agents "enhance" performance; they can, at most, enable performance. A pill cannot give a speech or play a symphony. Unlike steroids, perhaps, they cannot make you bigger and stronger so that you can hit a baseball harder and further. All they can possibly do is to dampen excessive anxiety to "keep you in the game." Alprazolam is a sedative. Beta blockers beyond optimal dose can be deadening, creating a robot-like sensation. Would anyone who regards these substances as "performance

---

[4] I haven't checked in with my office today but "handicap" is apparently outré and the currently politically correct term is "disability." That, of course, is backwards from any proper sense of the language. "Disability" implies that you can't do something; that you are not able to do it. "Handicapped," on the other hand, means you can do something but you have an impediment imposed upon you that makes it harder for you to do it than someone who is free of that particular handicap. This is why horses are "handicapped." (Mercifully, we don't "disable" them.) Some horses are sometimes made to carry more weight to make for a more exciting race. People with a "handicap" can, and do, apply extra effort and determination to reach the result that others might achieve without that heightened effort.

CHAPTER 14: CONCLUSIONS

enhancing" care to try them? No one who didn't need them would want to risk the sedation or deadening of these medications, nor would he find any enhancement from taking them.

My wife tells the story of being taught by an elementary school teacher who had no experience of allergies and, apparently, was a very stupid person as well. Because she had no personal experience of allergies, she summarily rejected my wife's protestations and insisted that she sit close to the flowers whenever they were brought to class, whether she sneezed her head off or not.

It makes no more sense to let people who are free of stagefright opine on what are appropriate approaches to managing it than it does to let my wife's grade school teacher dismiss her allergies as "only in your head."

Part of the title of this book is *Stagefright Solved*. By no means should that be taken as an expression that there is no further progress to be made. I am both certain and hopeful that there will be further beneficial advancements. I also firmly believe that progress is inevitable if we will only stay out of its way. By "solved" I mean that we have identified and confirmed — by more than a quarter of a century of practice — the cognitive patterns that initiate stagefright. We have also confirmed and perhaps elaborated on the seminal work of the Brantigans in describing its metabolic pathways. In addition, I have collected for you everything I have gathered from my own personal experience, my over twenty-five years of helping others, and everything else I have discovered that is likely to be helpful. Undoubtedly, over time, additional tools will become available for inclusion in the stagefright toolbox.

Since we implemented the Stagefright Survival School, I have had the pleasure of working with all kinds of people who share the fear of public speaking. A positive common thread is that the more they followed our curriculum, the more they were able to get a handle on their stagefright.

Some final thoughts: Use whatever resources you have at your disposal. If an opportunity to speak comes up at a small, casual gathering, you can use that as one of your practice sessions. It doesn't matter if there are just three people there; it's still a chance to practice speaking.

Take an active role in overcoming your fears. If you wait for a public-speaking opportunity to present itself, it might not happen for a while. Like anything, presenting while using our techniques will get easier with more practice.

Set achievable, positive goals, and remember to forgive yourself if you have a "setback." Blaming yourself will only make you feel worse and won't help you kick your stagefright.

CHAPTER 14: CONCLUSIONS

As you now know, the key to managing stagefright is to not think about yourself while speaking in public. Of course that's easier said than done. There is no magic cure for those of us who are challenged by stagefright, but with work and focus, it can be overcome. We hope you'll be able to use the tools we've provided to put your stagefright in the past, where it belongs.

POSTSCRIPT

THE STAGEFRIGHT SURVIVAL SCHOOL POST-GRADUATE COURSE

I have participated in Stagefright Survival School classes over the years primarily to brief students on medication information and their individualized options of what, if anything, to try. I always make the point that I consider the medications to be "training wheels" that enable and encourage our students to take the risk of placing themselves into practice speeches with more confidence. Repeated exposure to the phobic situation — public speaking events — is the key strategy that will bring success. If the medications help make a stagefright-sufferer feel more comfortable with stepping up more frequently to take on speaking opportunities, that's a good thing. And of course, I stress that everyone pay good attention to the guidance and the cognitive-behavioral strategies developed by Burt Rubin, our expert stagefright guru.

As a result of my involvement, I have met nearly all of our students over the years, hundreds of Washingtonians, as well as stagefright-sufferers from around the country. My relationship with some can last for years since I believe that if the medications continue to help, why not keep prescribing them for individuals who need them until they are ready to let them go? I am a firm believer in one key word: functionality.

I have gotten to follow up with some of our students over the course of several years. I have come to view these students as dealing with "The Last 10 Percent" — meaning, they typically have had big success in overcoming most of their extreme fear of public speaking, their stagefright, but there still may be a residual amount that bothers them. That pushed me to think through with them what could be added that would enable them to make further progress and finish the job.

Here's what I came up with: The first idea is what I term "The Training Effect."

Picture that you have decided to learn how to play golf. A friend advises you that the easiest way to begin is to go to a driving range, buy a bucket of balls and just start hitting balls onto the practice green.

The next Saturday you go and do just that. At first, you're plain missing the ball altogether. Then you're whacking the ball mainly inside the cage, mostly getting beaned by your own efforts. Then a few of your balls start traveling forward in the right direction. Then towards the end of your first practice session, the last few balls actually go kind of straight and even reach 20 feet onto the practice green.

POSTSCRIPT

The next Saturday, life happens, and you can't return. And so it goes for the next three Saturdays as well.

Finally, you're back, weeks later. You buy another bucket of balls — and guess what? You're back to square one. Bummer. Maybe by the end of this second session, you're just a little ahead of where you were at the end of your first session and it may take a little less time to get there.

Now, imagine that you were able to return the very next Saturday. You would still be starting off roughly at square one — but very soon after you begin hitting balls, you catch up with where you left off, and now you're making real progress. By the end of the second practice session, you're hitting them straight, and 75 yards out, too.

What's the difference? The training effect.

If there's too long a lapse in time between sessions, there's degradation of your training results. There's a decay curve.

The lesson?

To build on a learning curve, it's not just doing the practice that's important but also *the time interval* between the sessions. Wait too long, and you're always starting over from scratch. If you can make sure to keep the intervals short between your practices, you build up your learning curve much more effectively for making progress.

This approach runs counter to the most typical mental position of most phobics: *Avoidance*. Even though you may have graduated from the Stagefright Survival School and made much progress, avoidance tends to be a stubborn holdout. Sure, when opportunities come up for speaking events, you'll (somewhat grudgingly) accept them: "OK, I know I have to do it; Burt told me so."

Now, let's picture reframing the situation. Imagine that you take on overcoming stagefright as a personal mission to which you resolve to commit an entire year. I know that assumes that you are prepared to make a true commitment that will take priority over many other things. You decide to do it because it's a goal so important to you that you will not allow anything to get in its way.

Here's a personal example of that kind of mission: my decision early in college to become a doctor. Why a doctor? I'm not completely sure. Even knowing all the personal and family factors that led me to take on this goal, there's a mystery factor that I can't explain. It was just there. Be that as it may, I was determined that's what I wanted to do.

POSTSCRIPT

Studying pre-med meant I would have to take on fearsome Organic Chemistry as part of my course requirements. Very intimidating. I knew I would have to memorize a virtual telephone book of reactions, organic molecules, etc. And I would have to earn a top grade — or just forget medical school.

There was no alternative for me for the next year: Organic Chemistry with an A (or at worst, a B), or no med school. So I buckled down to grind my way through this required ordeal. Don't think I was in love with Organic Chemistry. But, by God, I did what I had to do, no matter the sacrifices involved.

I tell that story to demonstrate that if you promote something to be a top goal for yourself, and resolve to persevere towards it at any cost, for as long as it takes, maybe even for a full year or longer, you can do something you never believed you were capable of.

Now, I don't assume that everyone hearing my story necessarily has that kind of motivation for overcoming stagefright. Some people may decide it just isn't worth that much to them. And I understand that. But for the ones that really do want to overcome their stagefright — whatever it takes — my message seems to have had resonance.

I advise people to think about pulling a reverse move on their fear. Fears always have this powerful weapon at the ready: *Avoidance*. What would happen if, instead of avoiding public speaking situations, you resolve to actually *seek out* opportunities to speak? Not just wait for invitations to speak and then grudgingly do them (better than not doing them at all), but actually seek them out proactively? That would be totally upside down for you, a real break from your customary position.

Now, who will be in charge? *You* are — not your fear!

It's quite a reversal to seize back the power from your fear and actually proactively look for opportunities to speak in public. Or for you to create opportunities for public speaking that you invent yourself. Most of our students work in organizations that have room not only for scheduled speaking events but also for unscheduled events that you can whip up just for shortening the intervals between your practices.

You may come to be regarded as a grandstander who just loves attention and the limelight.

Who cares?

No one needs to know that you're still plenty scared and you're doing it primarily because you made a commitment to yourself that overcoming stagefright is going to be a top priority in your life for at least the next year.

This is what Burt has described as paradoxical: The very thing you fear is the very thing you seek to do as much as possible.

I've given this pep talk to scores of people that have come in to meet with me, sometimes several years after graduating from the Stagefright Survival School, and they only came in for a renewal of their prescriptions. I think a fair number have taken my words to heart and have pushed through their "Last 10 Percent."

Give this some thought.

People who buy into this idea come back later and proudly tell me about getting through their Last 10 Percent. They are truly euphoric at the freedom and results they have achieved.

Finally, if you want to experience the fullest benefit of our Stagefright Survival Program in Alexandria, Virginia, and have the opportunity to work directly with Burt Rubin, call: 703-836-7130 or 877-657-8243, or visit our website: www.StagefrightSurvival.com

Finally, as they say in show biz — break a leg!

Best of luck!

Dr. Charney

GLOSSARY

Alprazolam
A prescription drug useful in managing stagefright and anticipatory anxiety.

Anticipatory anxiety
Anxiety experienced in advance of a presentation caused by thinking about and picturing it.

Beta blockers
The family of chemicals available as prescription drugs that block the effect of catecholamines at beta adrenergic receptor sites where the catecholamines would need to attach to initiate the fight or flight response.

Catecholamines
The family of chemicals that include adrenaline that are released into the blood as hormones and act within the nervous system as neurotransmitters that initiate the fight or flight response.

Cognitive patterns of stagefright
The thought patterns that include thinking you will embarrass yourself and the self-conscious awareness that causes the release of catecholamines initiating the fight or flight response leading to stagefright.

Distraction techniques
The techniques set forth in Chapter 4 for distracting yourself from thinking about yourself so that you don't produce the catecholamines that cause stagefright.

Fear-thought
A thought or self-conscious awareness of embarrassing yourself that initiates the release of catecholamines.

Fight-or-Flight
The built-in bodily mechanisms that enable an animal to rapidly shift into effective survival mode for dealing with life-threatening situations. This includes neuronal and hormonal surges that prepare the animal for immediate corrective action, either for fleeing a predator or standing and fighting back.

Perfectionism
An unreasonable and unattainable standard of performance that refuses to accept any flaw, including appearing a little nervous.

Placebo
A physiologically inert treatment that will convince about 30 percent of people that it has a beneficial effect solely because they believe it is effective.

Prompting
A written word or phrase that you must see in front of you when you give a presentation to remind you to use a chosen distraction technique.

Propranolol
A member of the beta blocker family of prescription drugs.

Public speaking
Public speaking is oral communication any time you feel that you are "on," that is, the focus of attention, even if only one other person is present.

Toastmasters International
An organization for developing public speaking and leadership skills.

ABOUT THE AUTHORS

Burton Rubin, J.D.
Program Director

Burton Jay Rubin is the Director of the Stagefright Survival School. Burt earned his J.D. from the University of North Carolina Law School at Chapel Hill in 1969. He is a practicing attorney and has served as General Counsel for the American Society of Travel Agents. Burt also serves as a Commissioner on the utility providing water to 1.7 million people throughout Northern Virginia.

While Burt keeps busy at his "day jobs," he is passionate about helping people with fear of public speaking. It is a problem he knows well because for years he struggled with stagefright himself until he overcame it by using many of the techniques that are now taught by the Stagefright Survival School. His warmth, grace and wit make it easy for him to pass along the lessons he has learned for himself.

Burt is also the Director of the Fear of Flying Program for the Roundhouse Square Counseling Center.

David L. Charney, M.D.
CEO and Medical Consultant

David L. Charney, M.D., is a psychiatrist and is the founder and Medical Director of the Roundhouse Square Counseling Center. He earned his medical degree at the Upstate Medical Center, State University of New York, in Syracuse, then served in the United States Air Force for two years before starting his private psychiatry practice in Alexandria, Virginia.

Dr. Charney is also a consultant for the United States intelligence community. He has worked with a number of high-profile spies and, based on his unique knowledge, has lectured about his findings to intelligence professionals in many settings. He has published two white papers on the subject.

Dr. Charney has enjoyed helping hundreds of people get over their fear of public speaking by prescribing medication to enhance the cognitive-behavioral techniques that are the mainstay of the Stagefright Survival School.

Made in the USA
Middletown, DE
22 March 2024